12 STEP THEMED
COLORING
BOOK

12 Step Slogans

Motivational Quotes

Positive Sayings

Mindfulness Activites

*Includes over
48 coloring pages and
48 lined journal pages*

NOTES:

If you would like to use this as a journal, colored pencils work best for the artwork because markers will bleed through on the back of each page.

If you decide to use markers, place a blank sheet of paper or cardstock behind the artwork to prevent color bleeding on the next coloring page.

We extended most of the coloring pages to the edge. This will allow you to remove a page and trim it to fit a standard frame. An 8" x 10" frame works best!

CHECK OUT OUR COLLECTION OF COLORING BOOKS AND JOURNALS

PROPERTY OF:

_____

CONTACT INFORMATION

_____

DATE

HONESTY

HOPE

FAITH

COURAGE

INTEGRITY

WILLINGNESS

HUMILITY

LOVE

DISCIPLINE

PATIENCE & PERSERVERENCE

AWARENESS

SERVICE

ISBN 9798396601437

Peace Joy Serenity

live MORE worry LESS

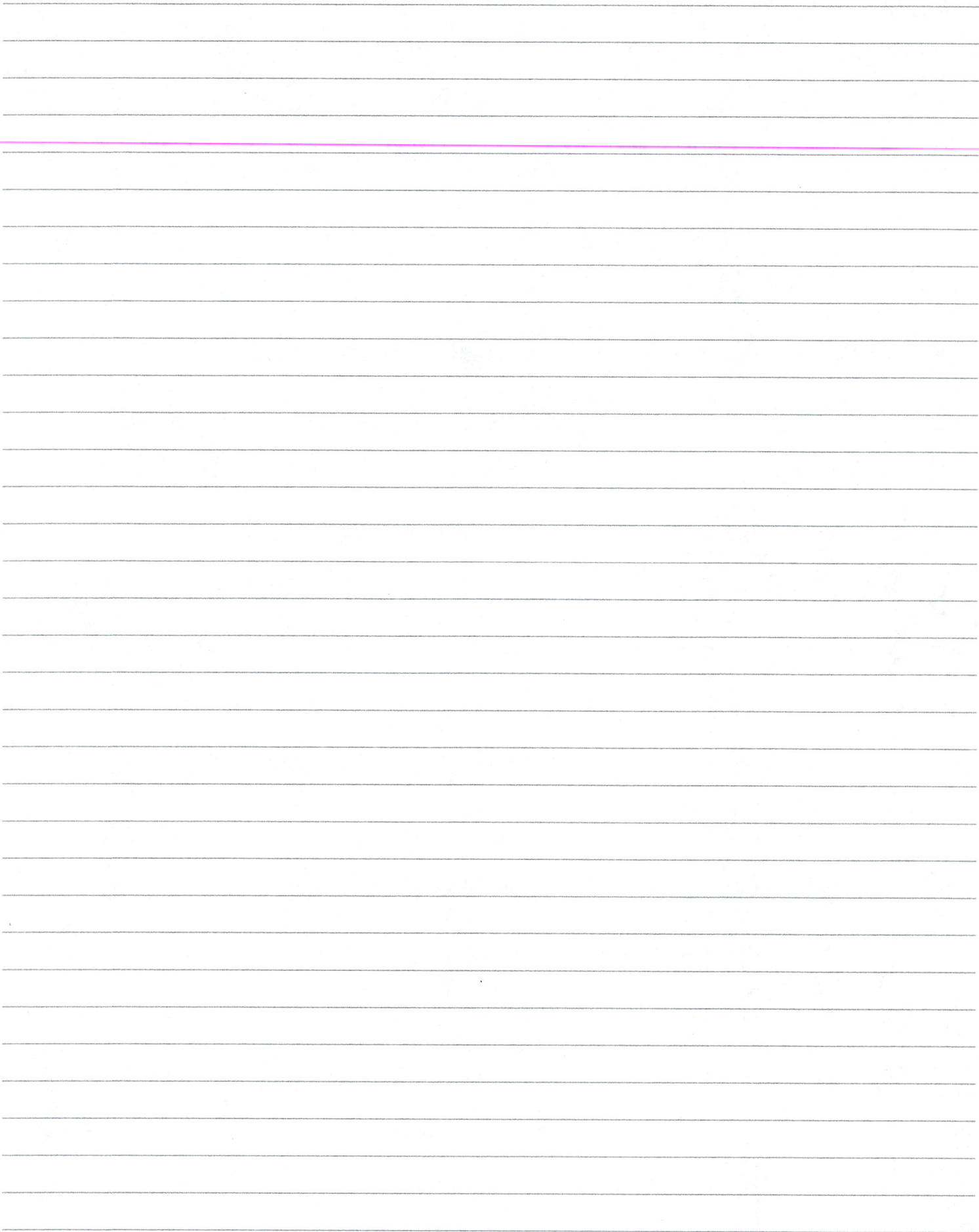

Do it because
it is in your heart...
Not because you
want something
in return.
SOCRATES

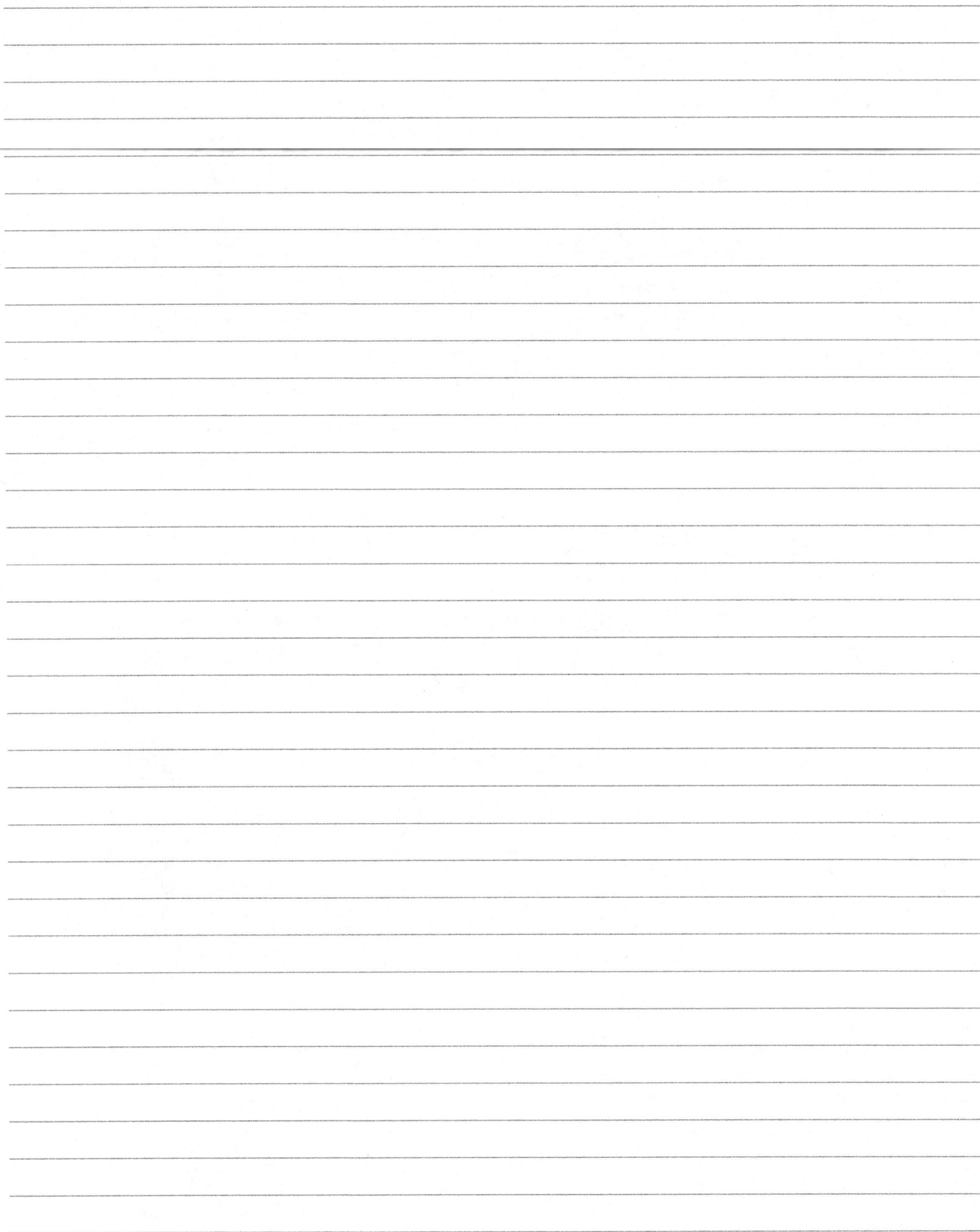

THE BEST IS YET TO COME

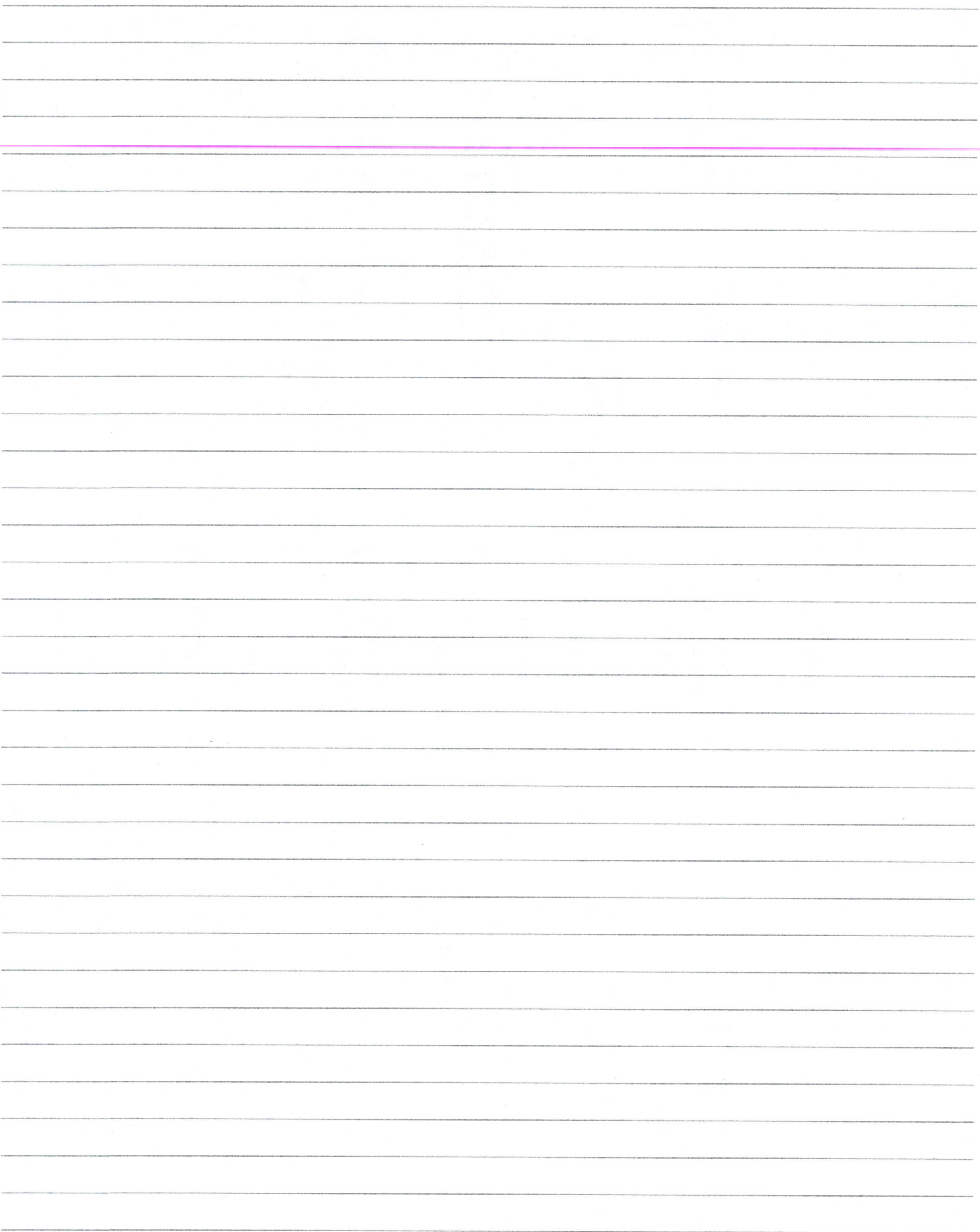

never
deprive
someone
of hope

*it might
be all
they have*

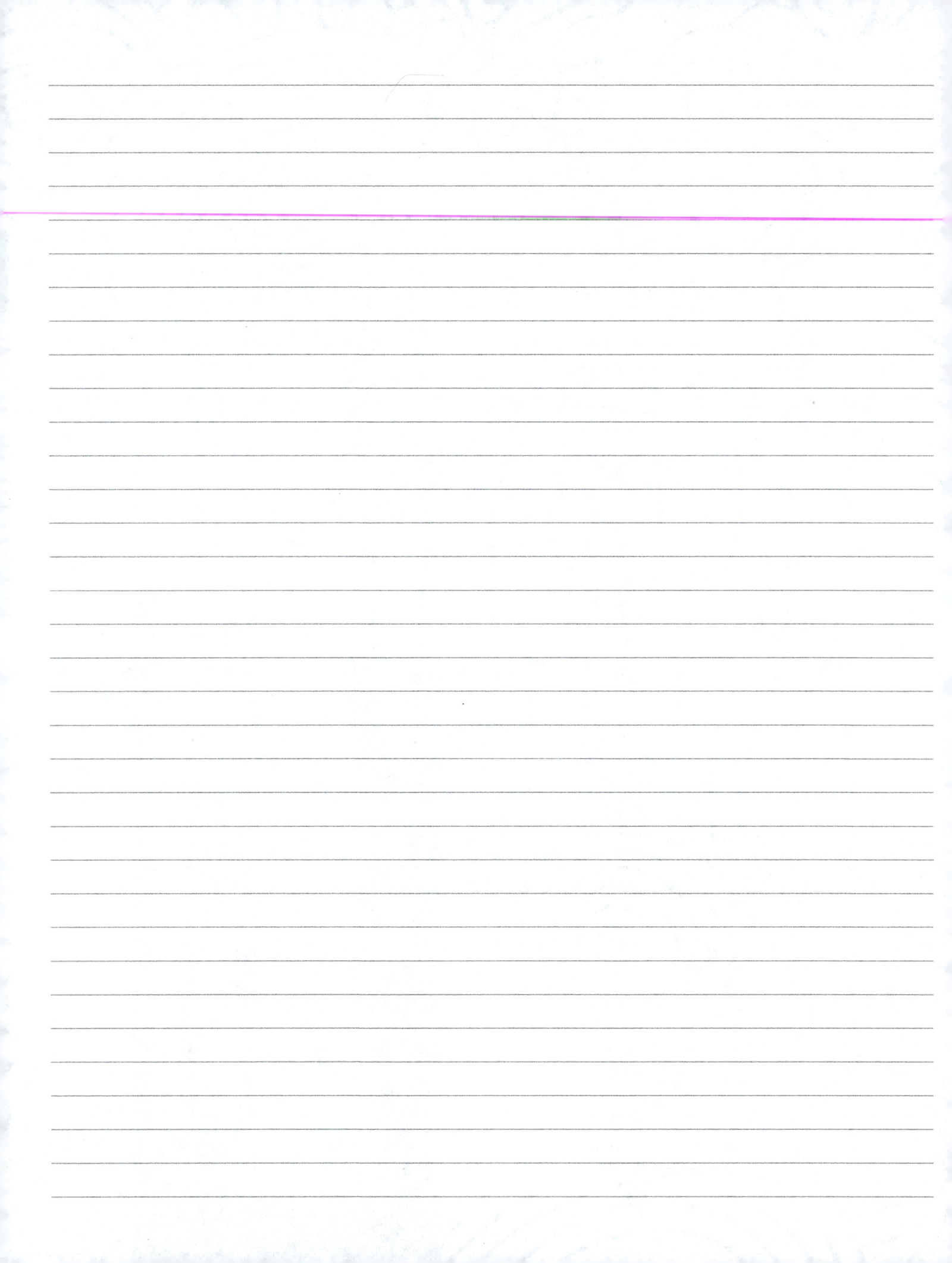

today is a good day for a good day

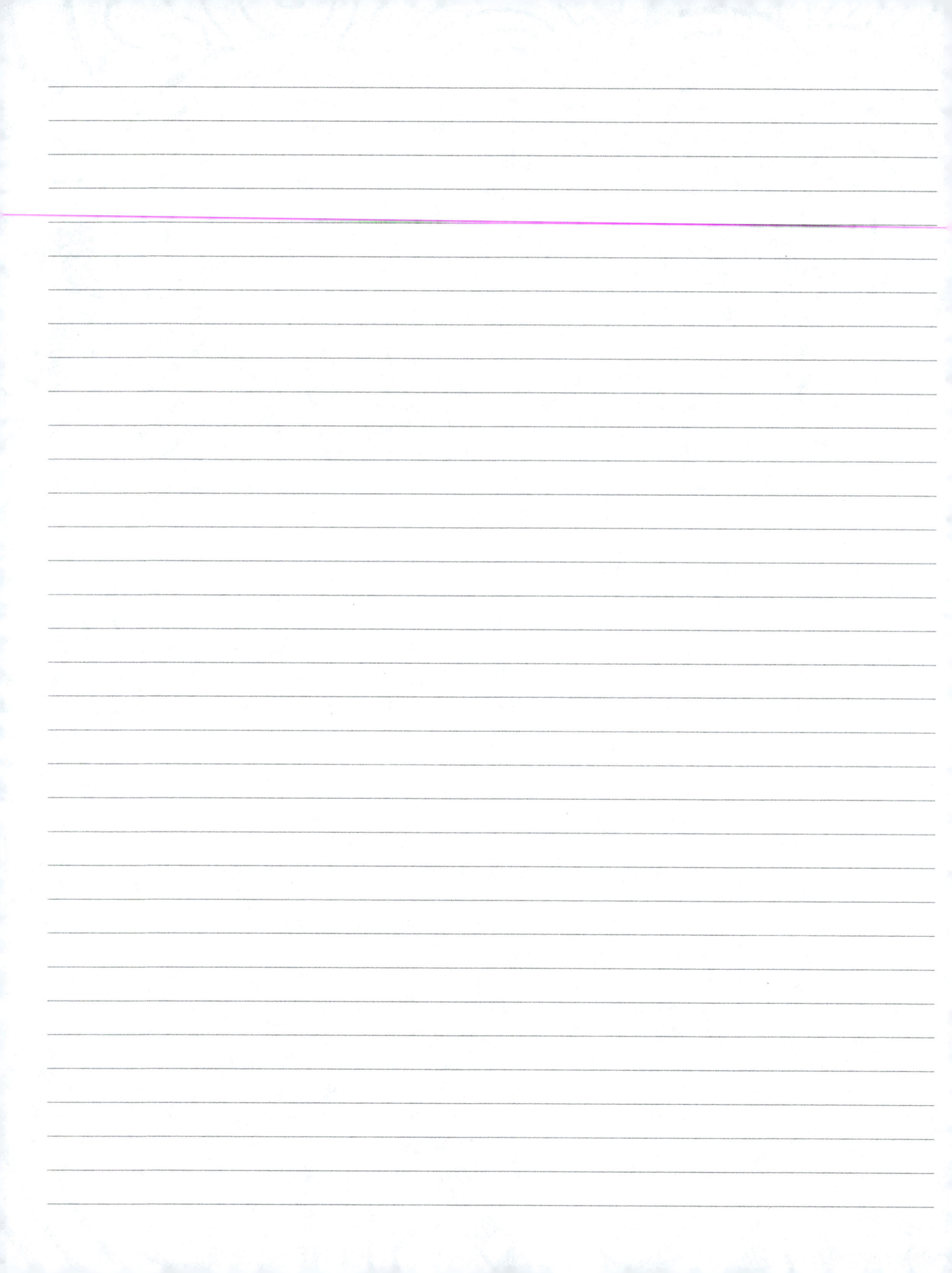

Never underestimate the power of a kind word or deed.

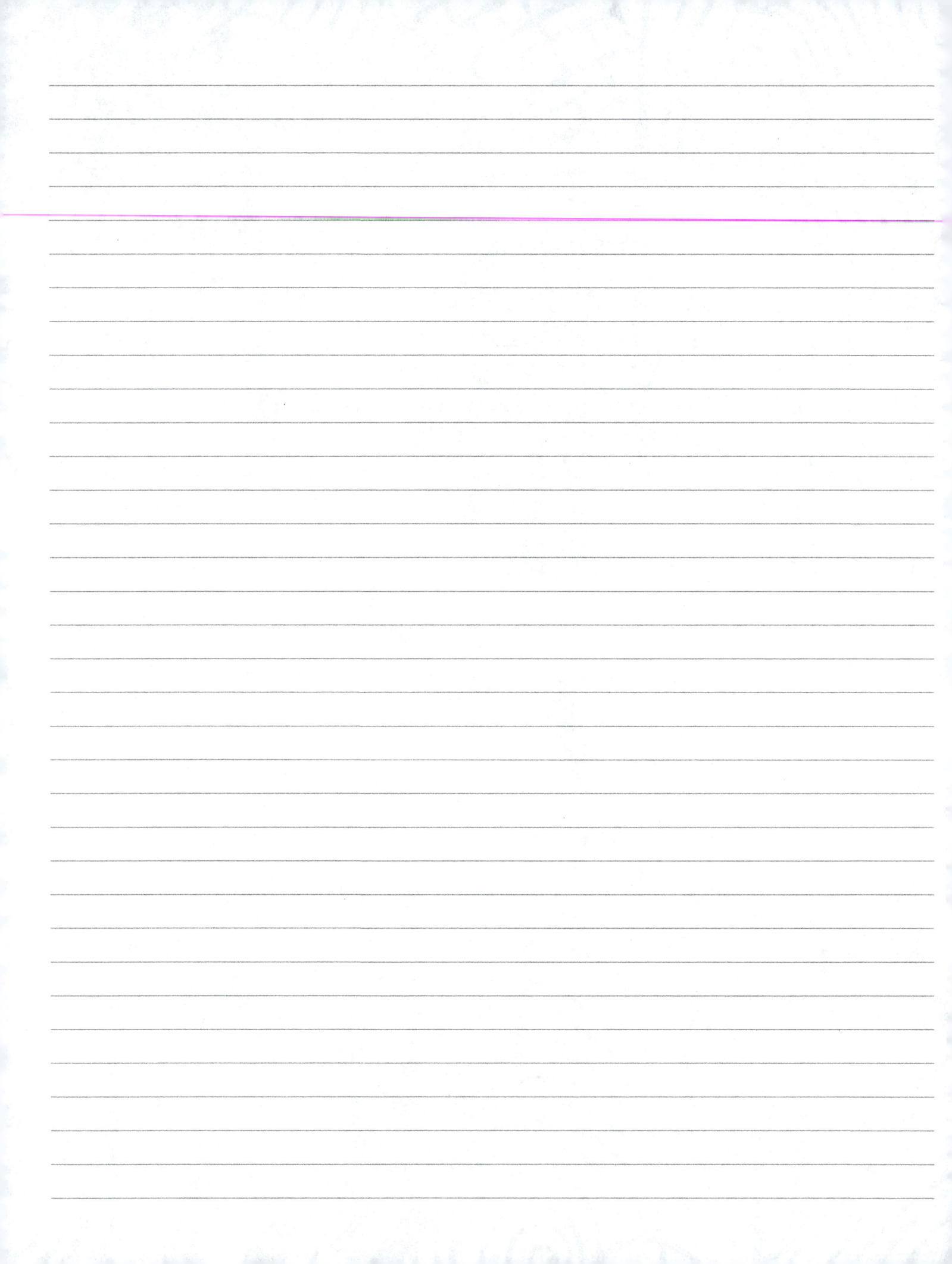

GOD, GRANT ME THE SERENITY TO ACCEPT THE THINGS I CANNOT CHANGE, THE COURAGE TO CHANGE THE THINGS I CAN, AND THE WISDOM TO KNOW THE DIFFERENCE.

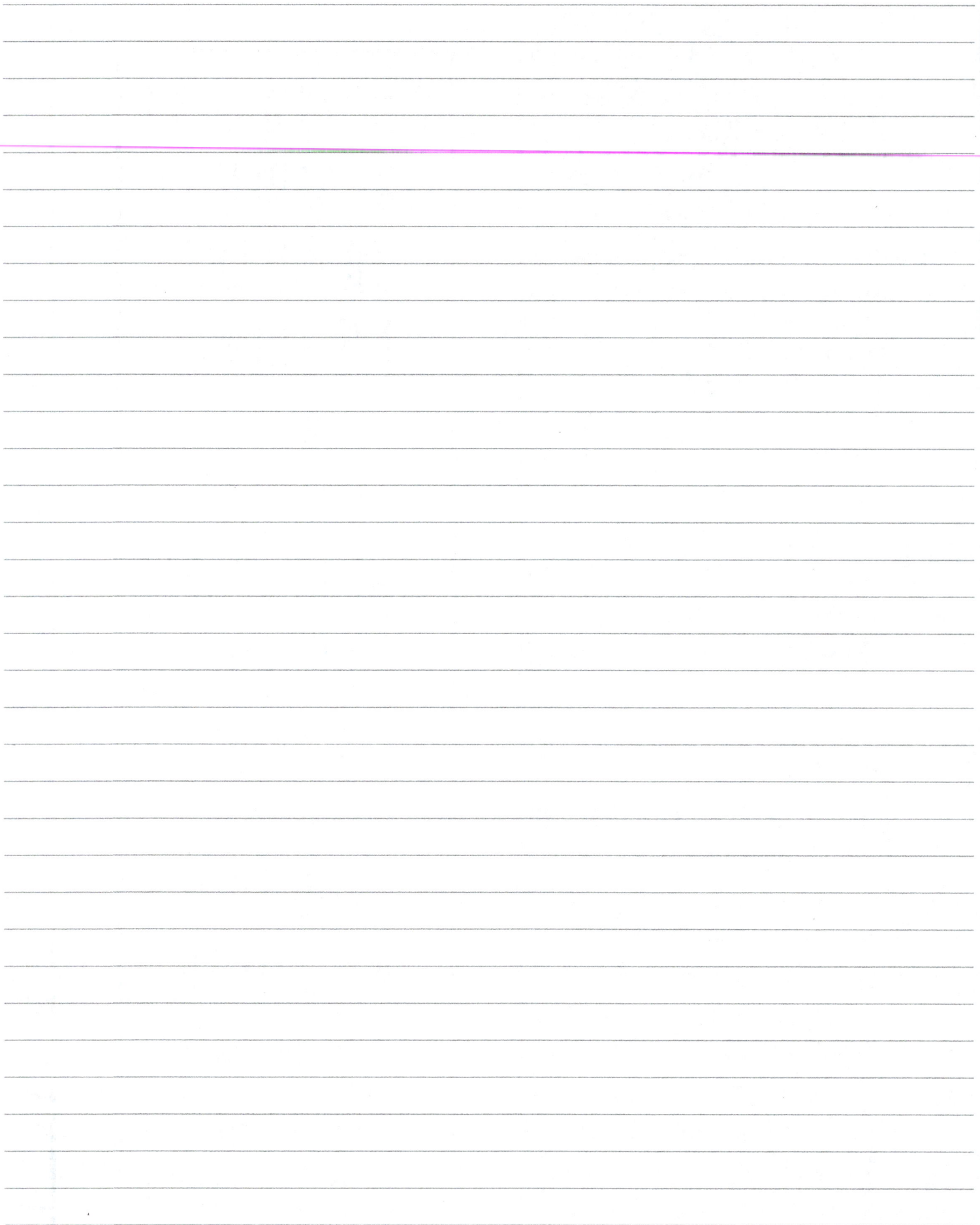

YOU CAN LEARN GREAT THINGS FROM YOUR MISTAKES WHEN YOU AREN'T BUSY DENYING THEM.

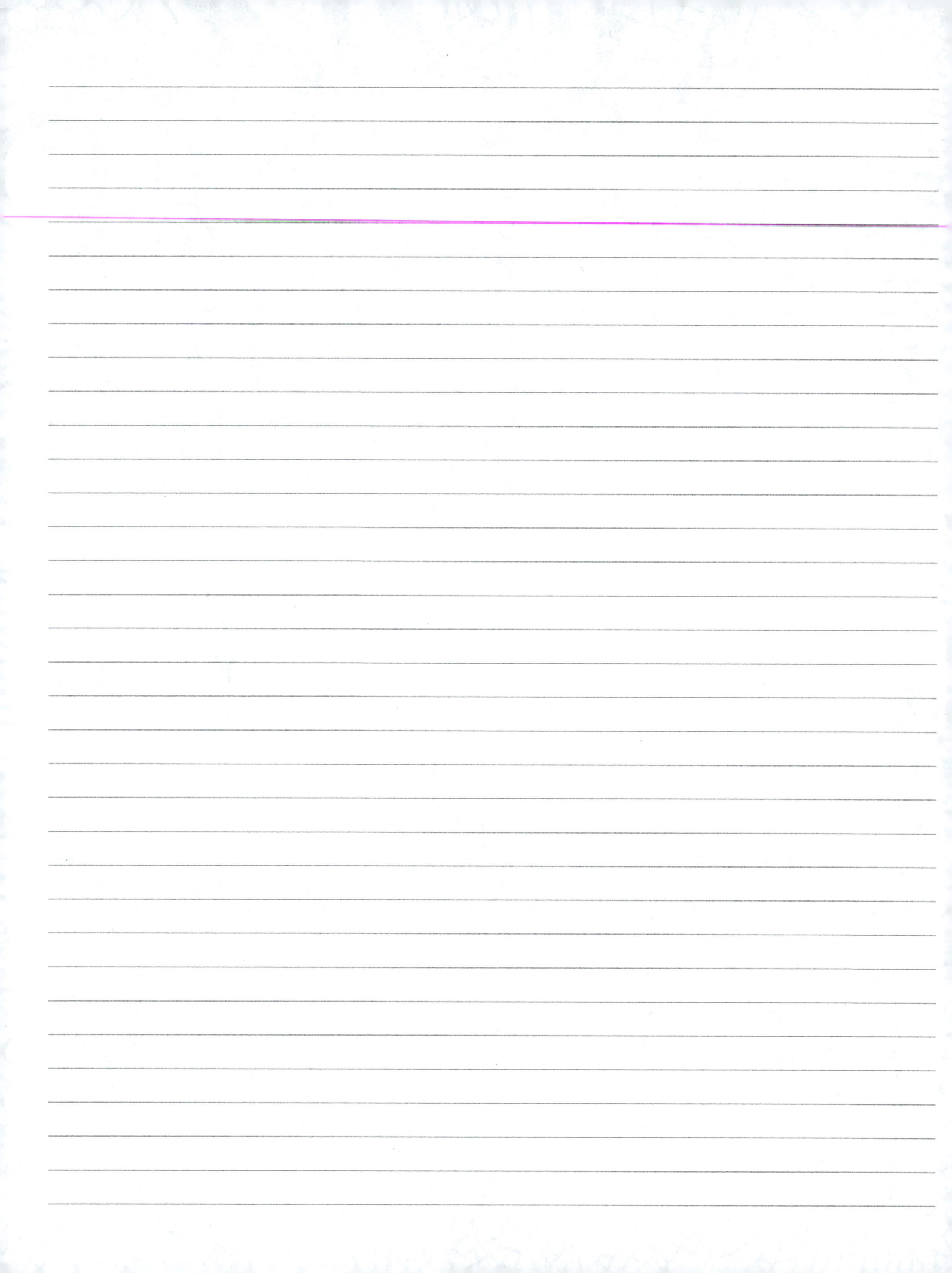

find joy in the journey

EXPECTATION IS THE ROOT OF ALL HEARTACHE.

SHAKESPEARE

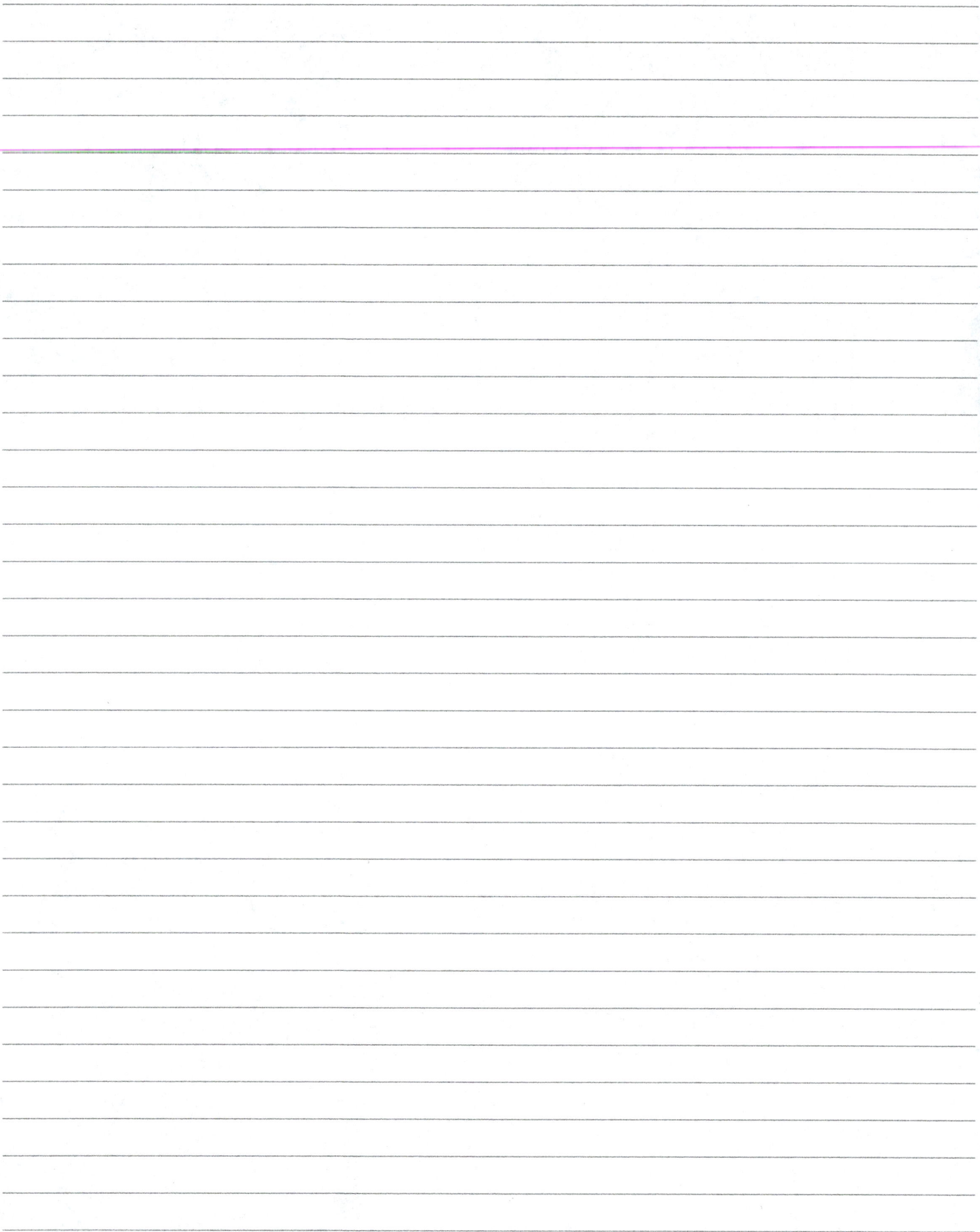

a smile is the prettiest thing you can wear

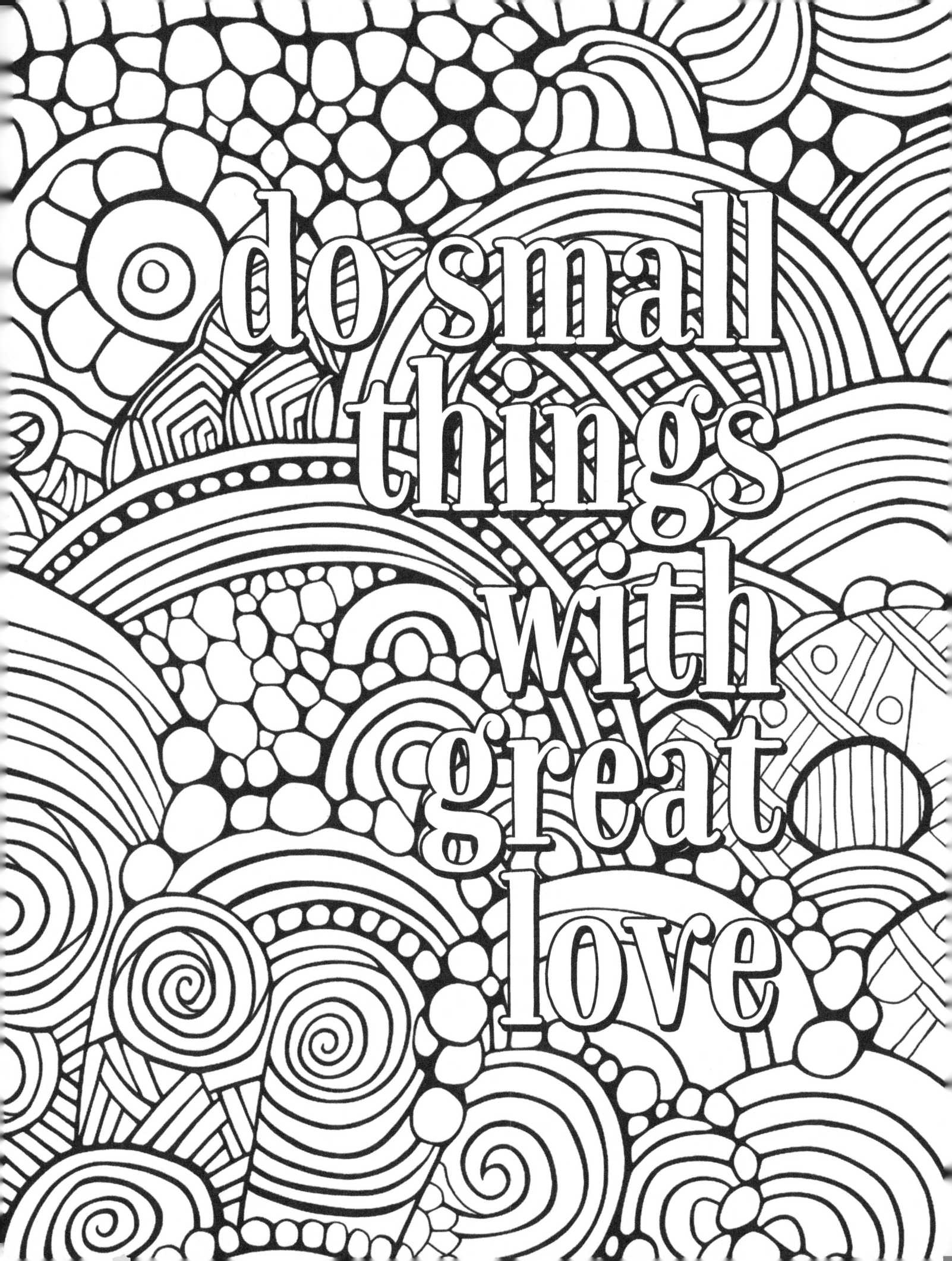

do small things with great love

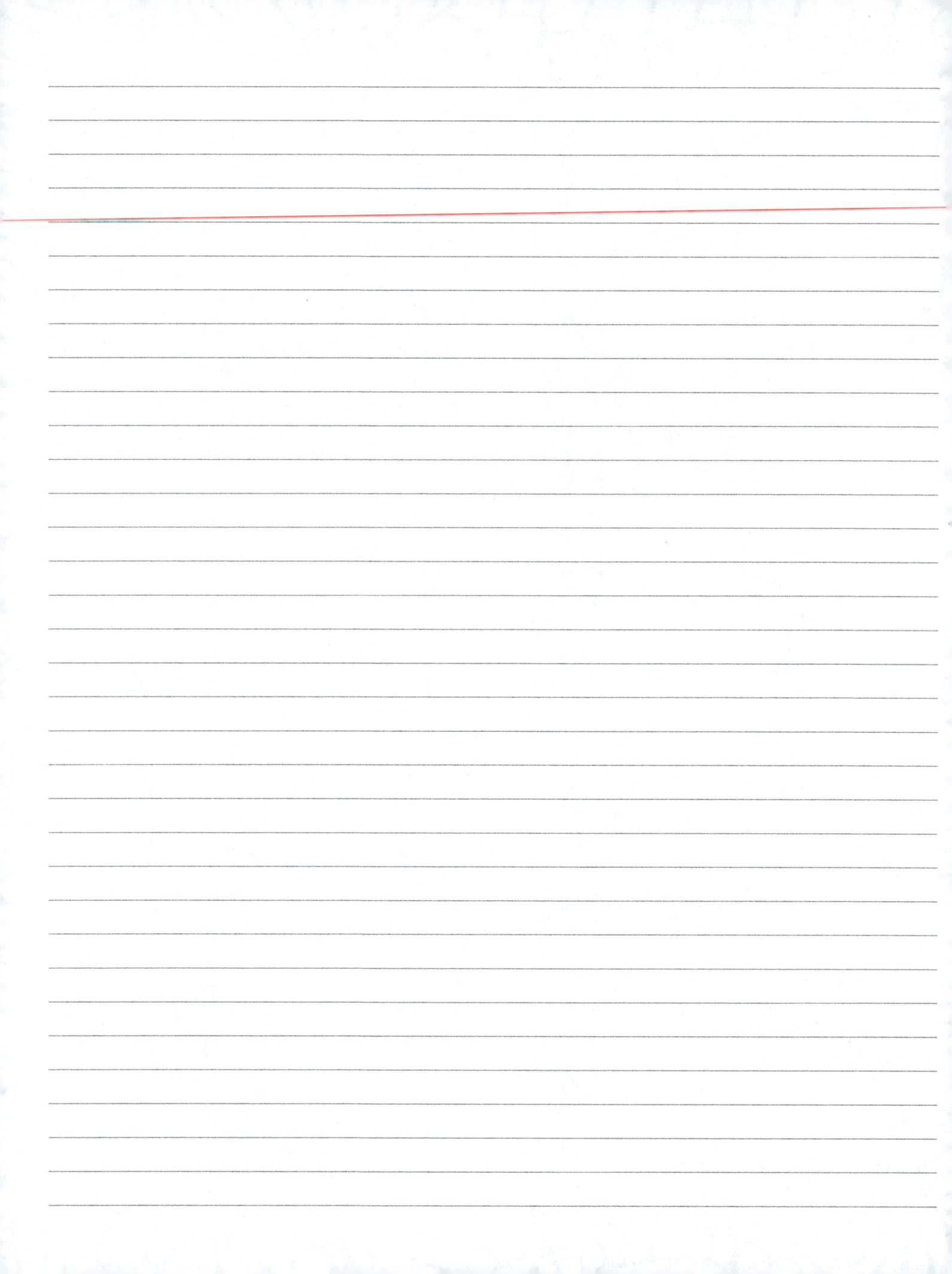

A SHORTCOMING
is like a flat tire.
A CHARACTER DEFECT
is like driving on it.

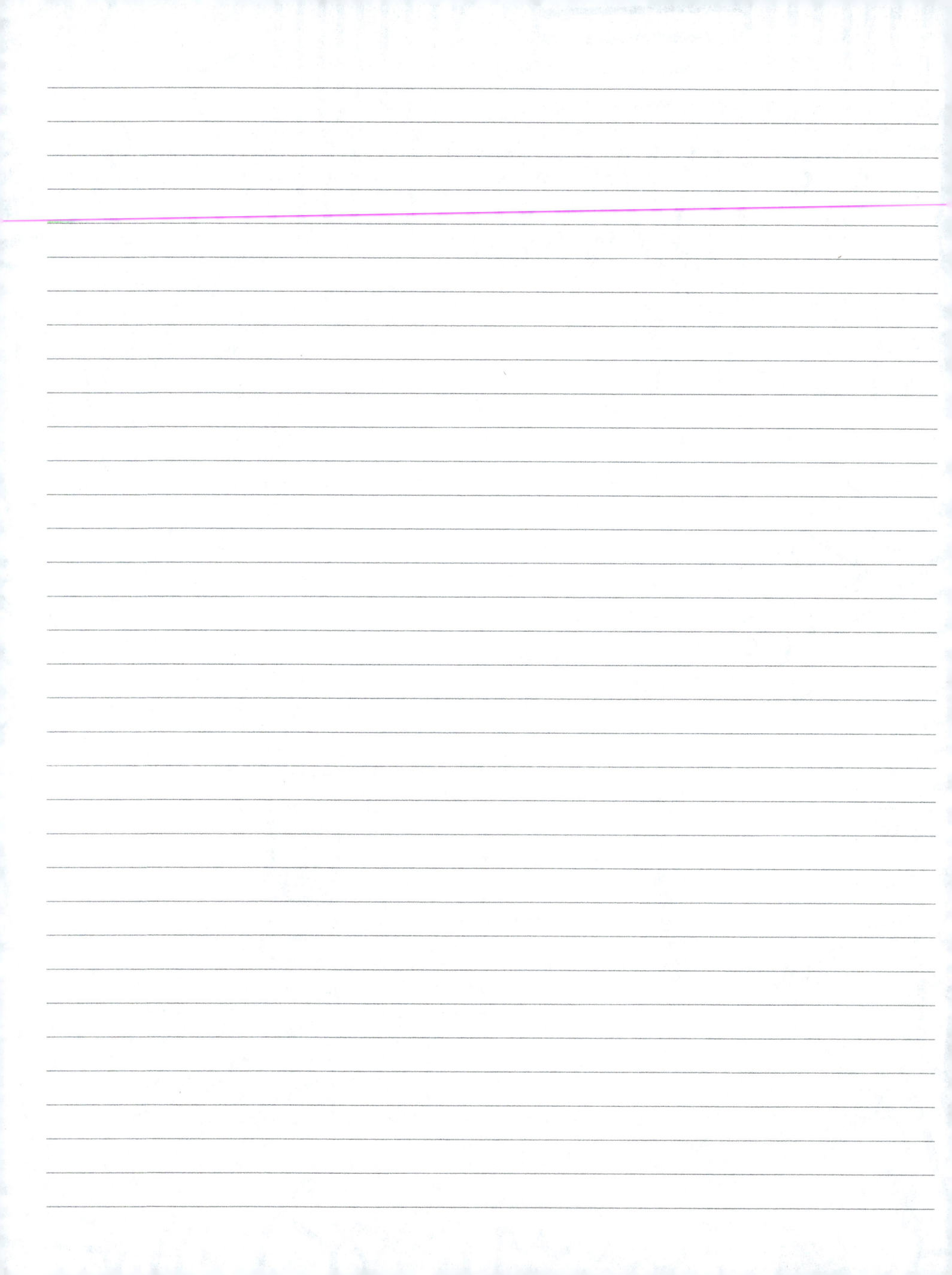

it is well with my soul

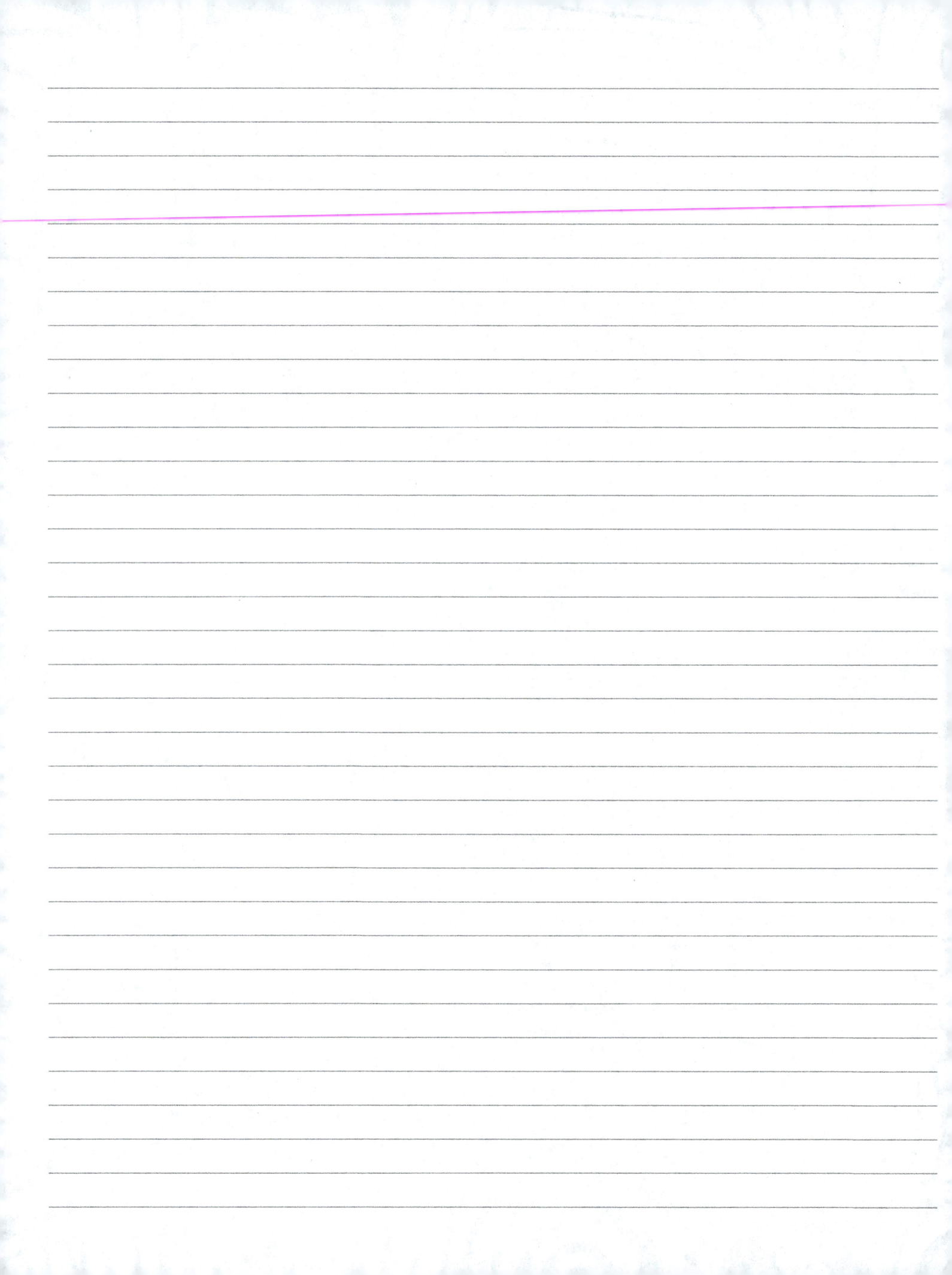

seek out the good in people

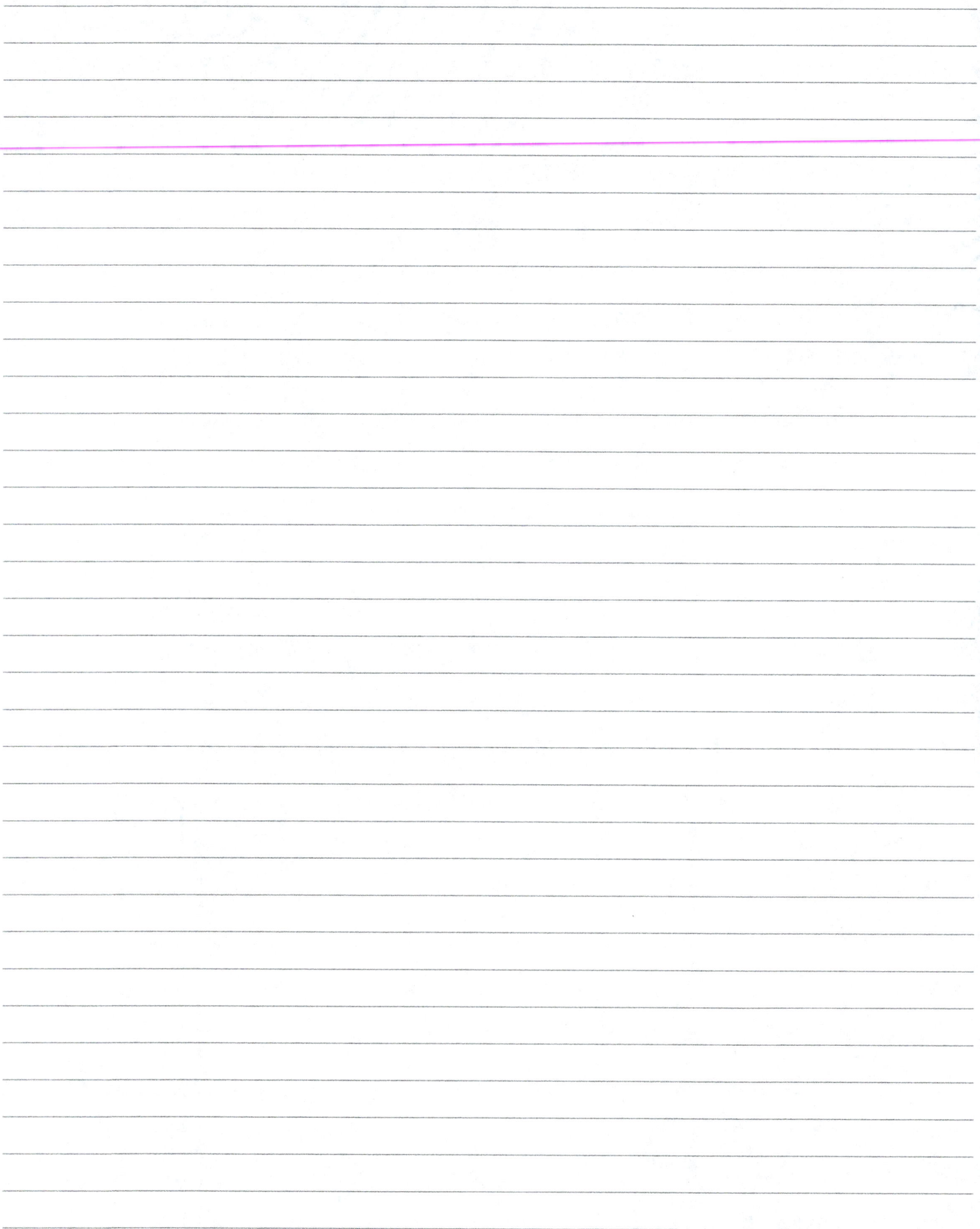

A lack of
boundaries
invites a
lack of
respect

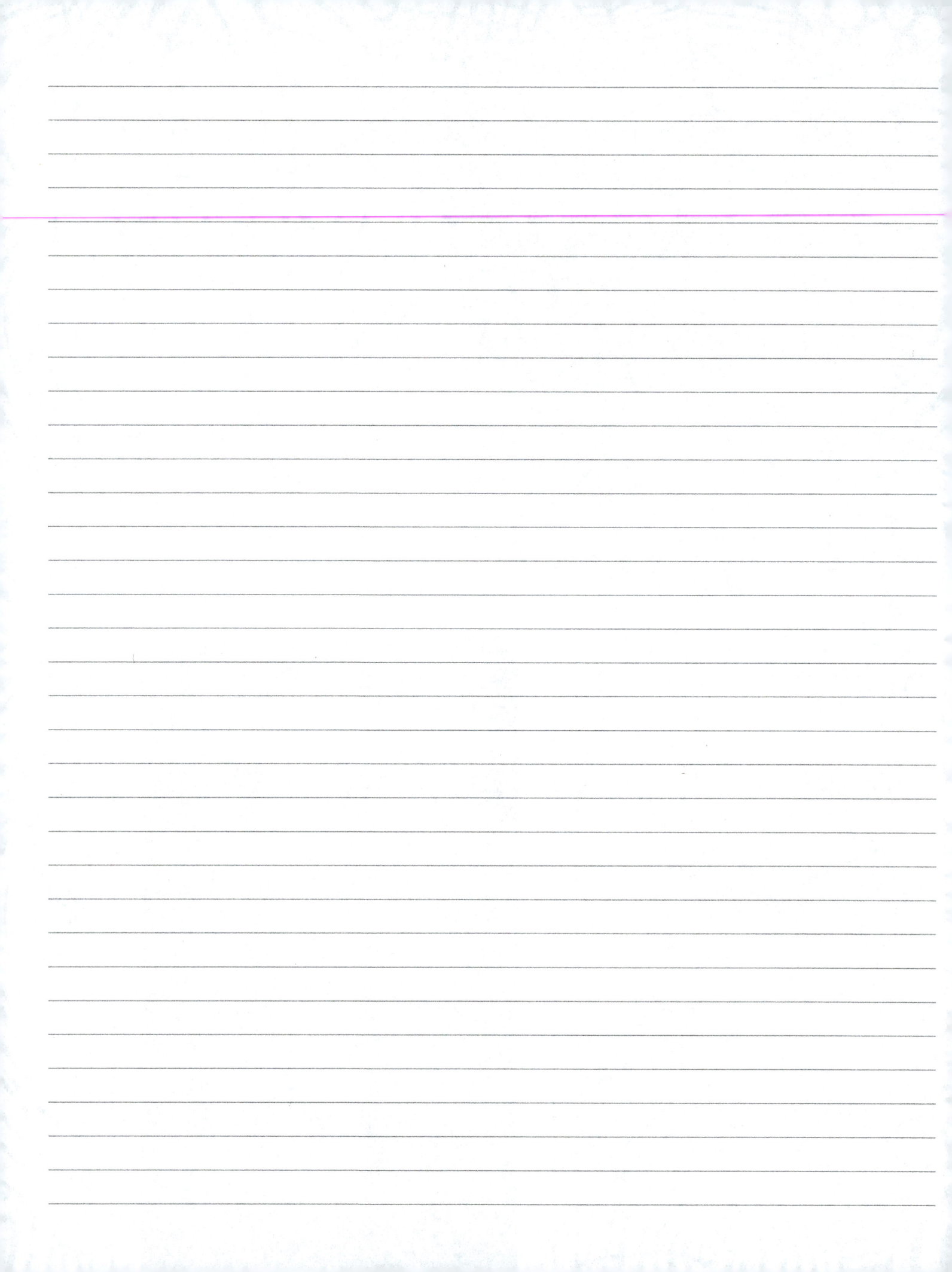

To Thine Own Self Be True

You are not a
human being
in search of a
spiritual
experience.
———
You are a
spiritual being
immersed in a
human
experience.

PIERRE TEILHARD de CHARDIN

FAITH IS THE OPPOSITE OF FEAR

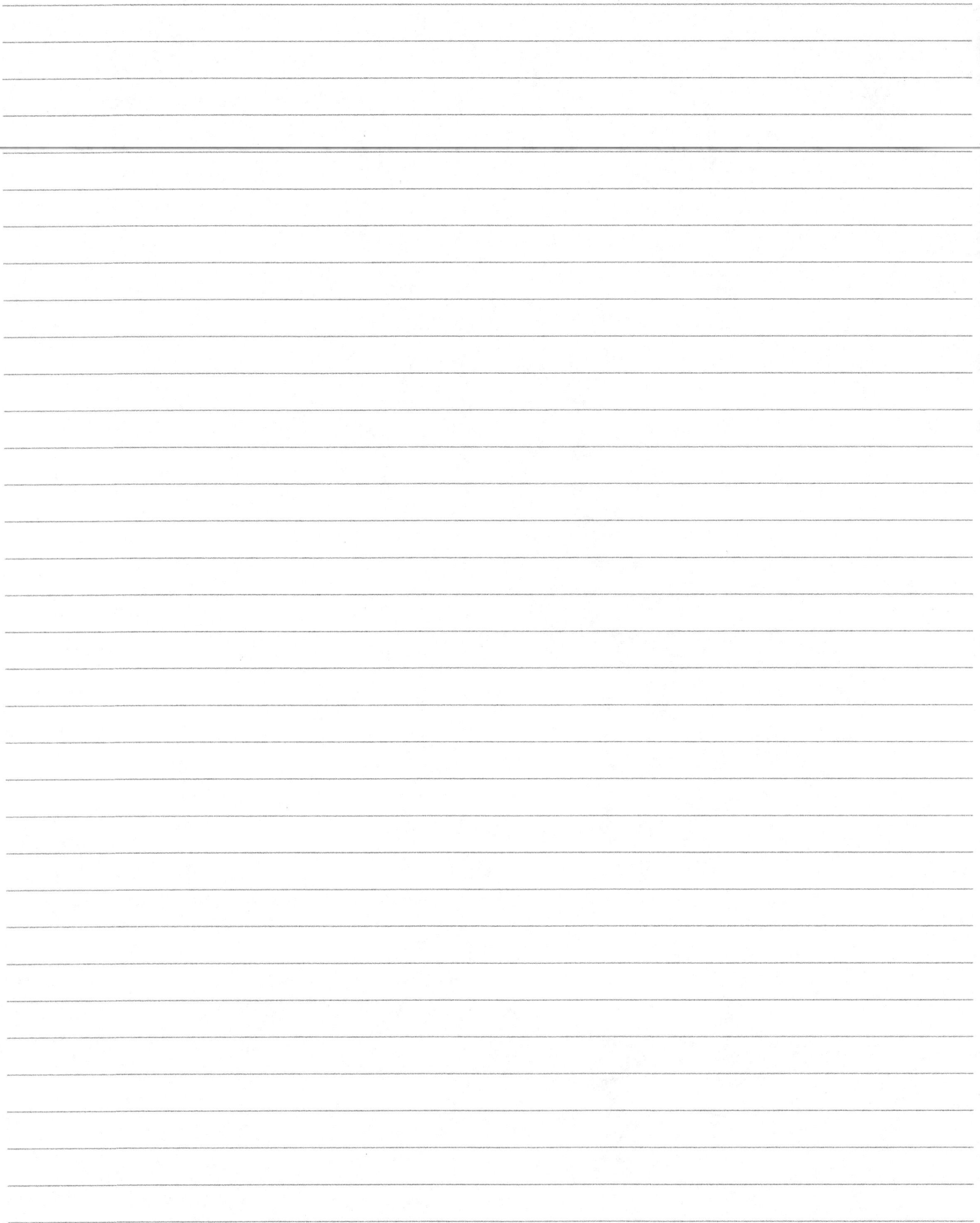

TWO THINGS YOU CAN CONTROL YOUR ATTITUDE & YOUR EFFORT

gratitude
IS AN
attitude

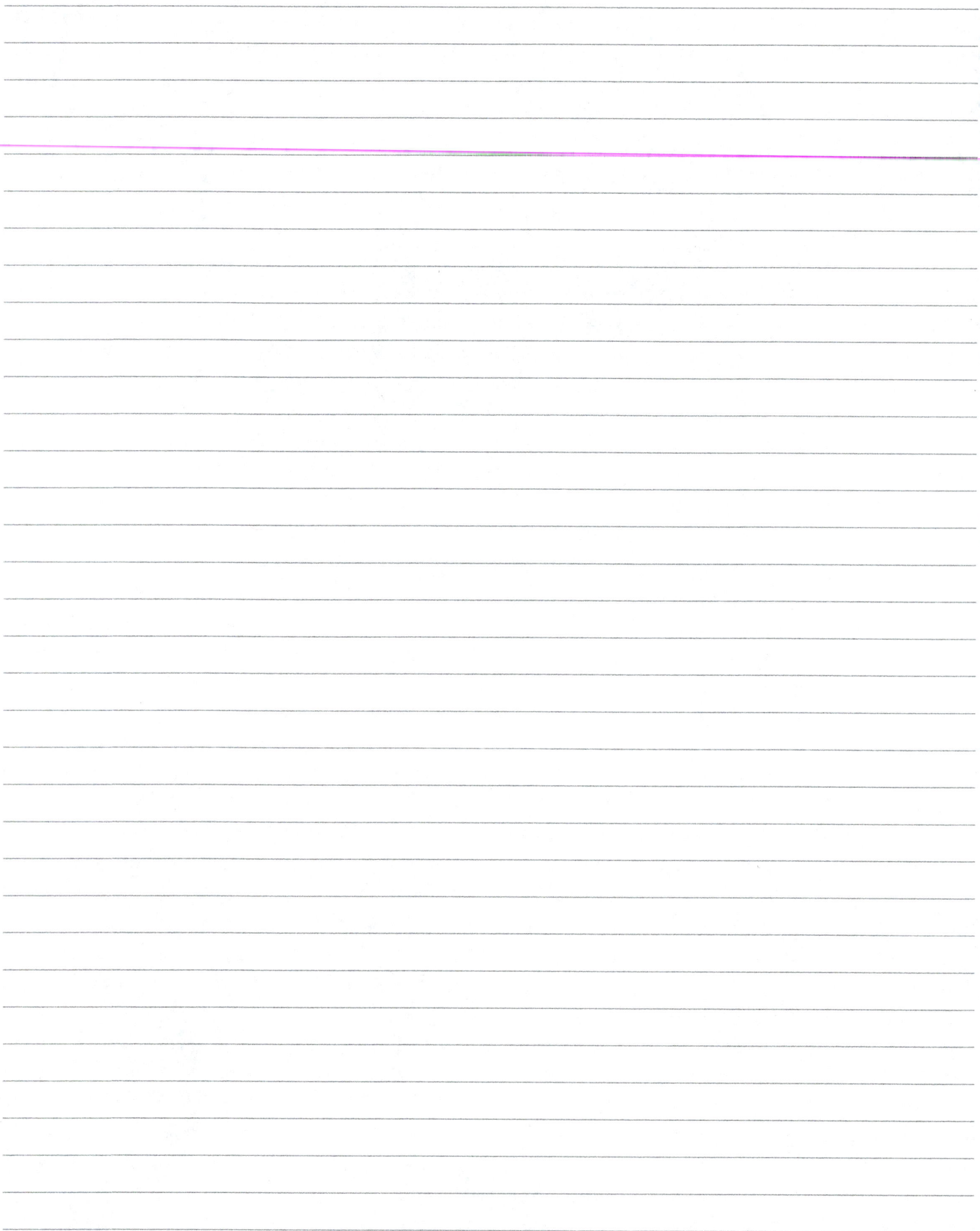

BE FORGIVING OF YOURSELF AND OTHERS

NOTHING CHANGES IF NOTHING CHANGES

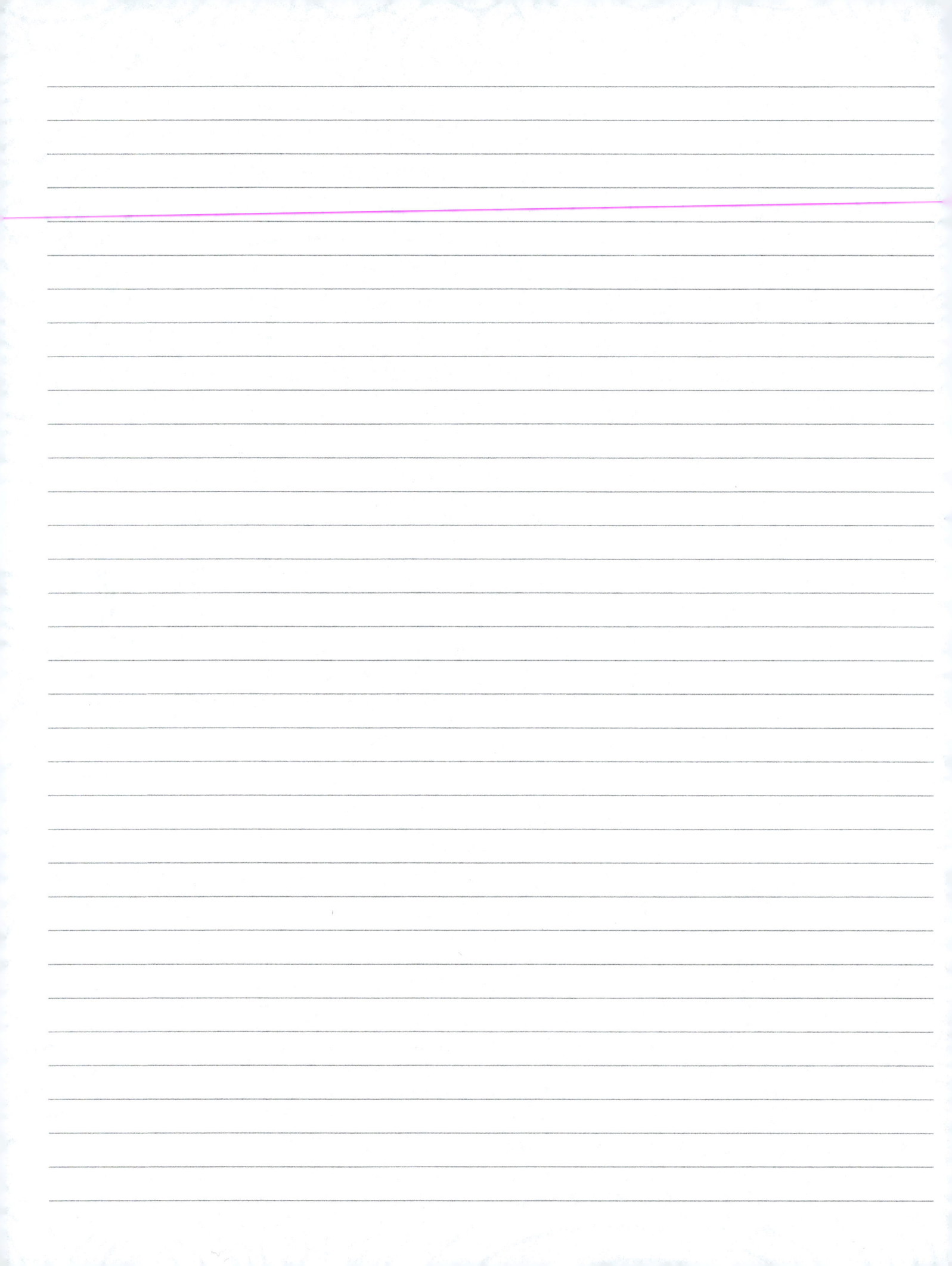

The day you plant the seed is not the day you eat the fruit

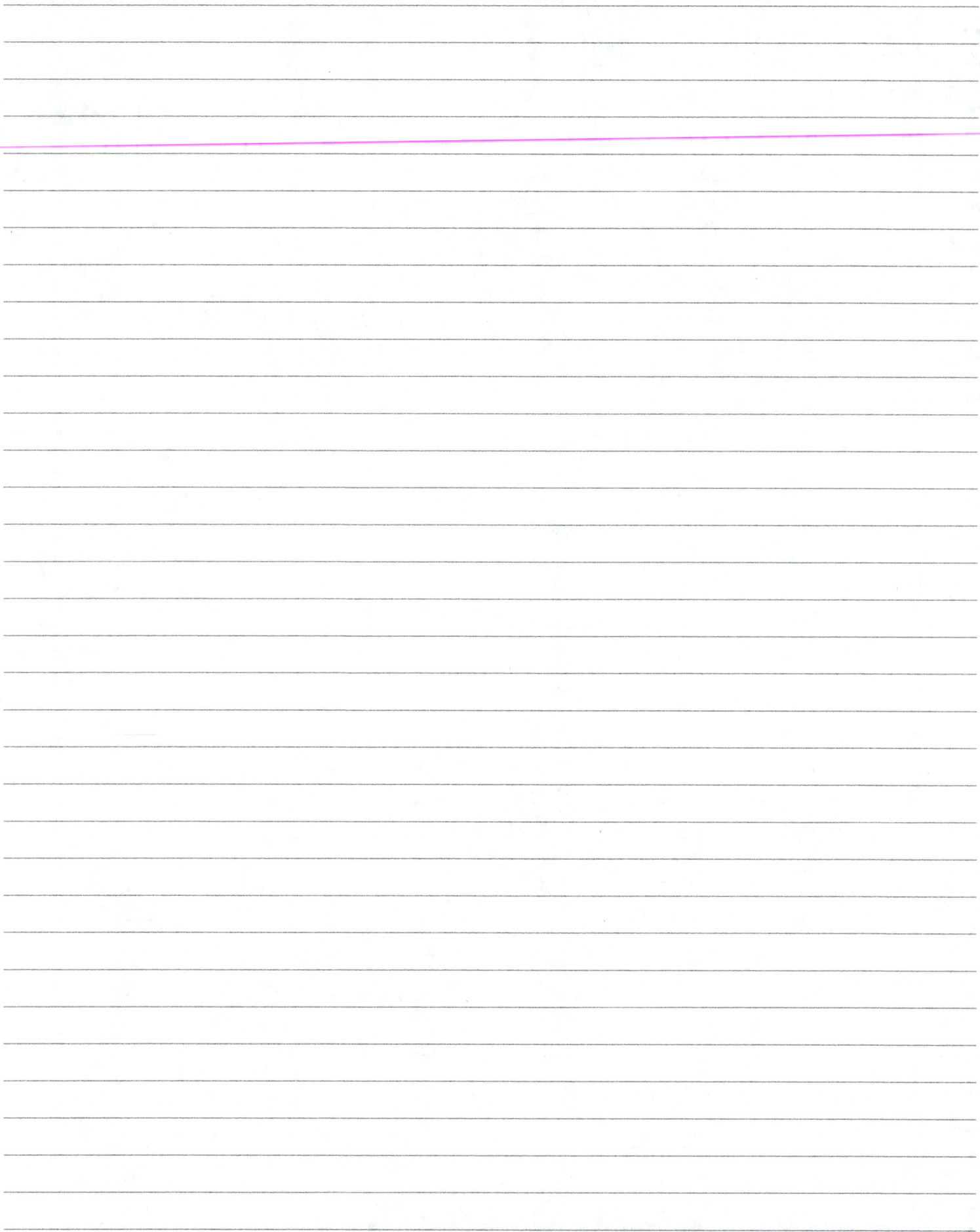

It's not happiness that brings you gratitude. It's gratitude that brings you happiness.

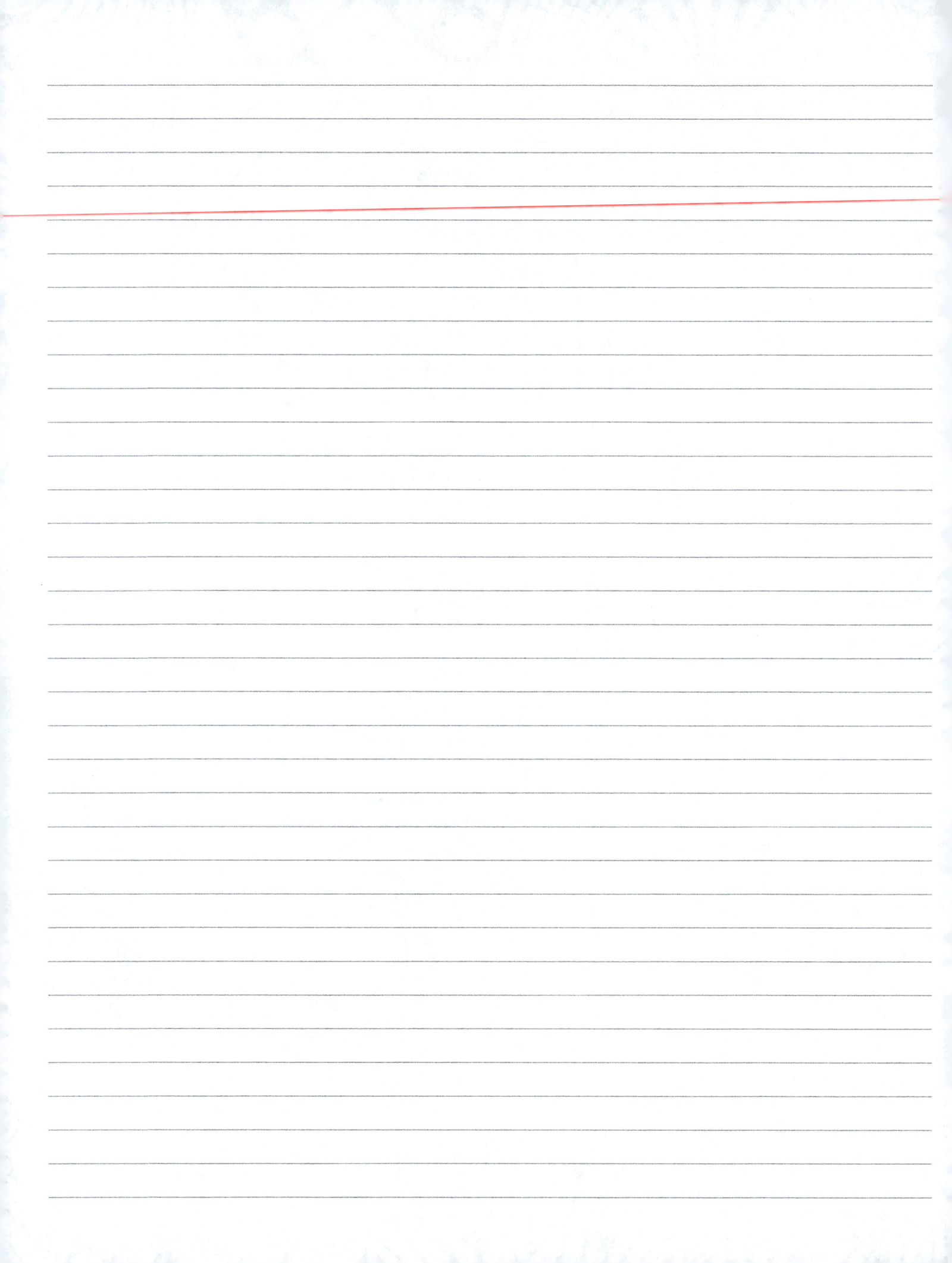

and so the adventure begins

PROGRESS
NOT
PERFECTION

YOU ARE
enough

Never underestimate the power to change yourself

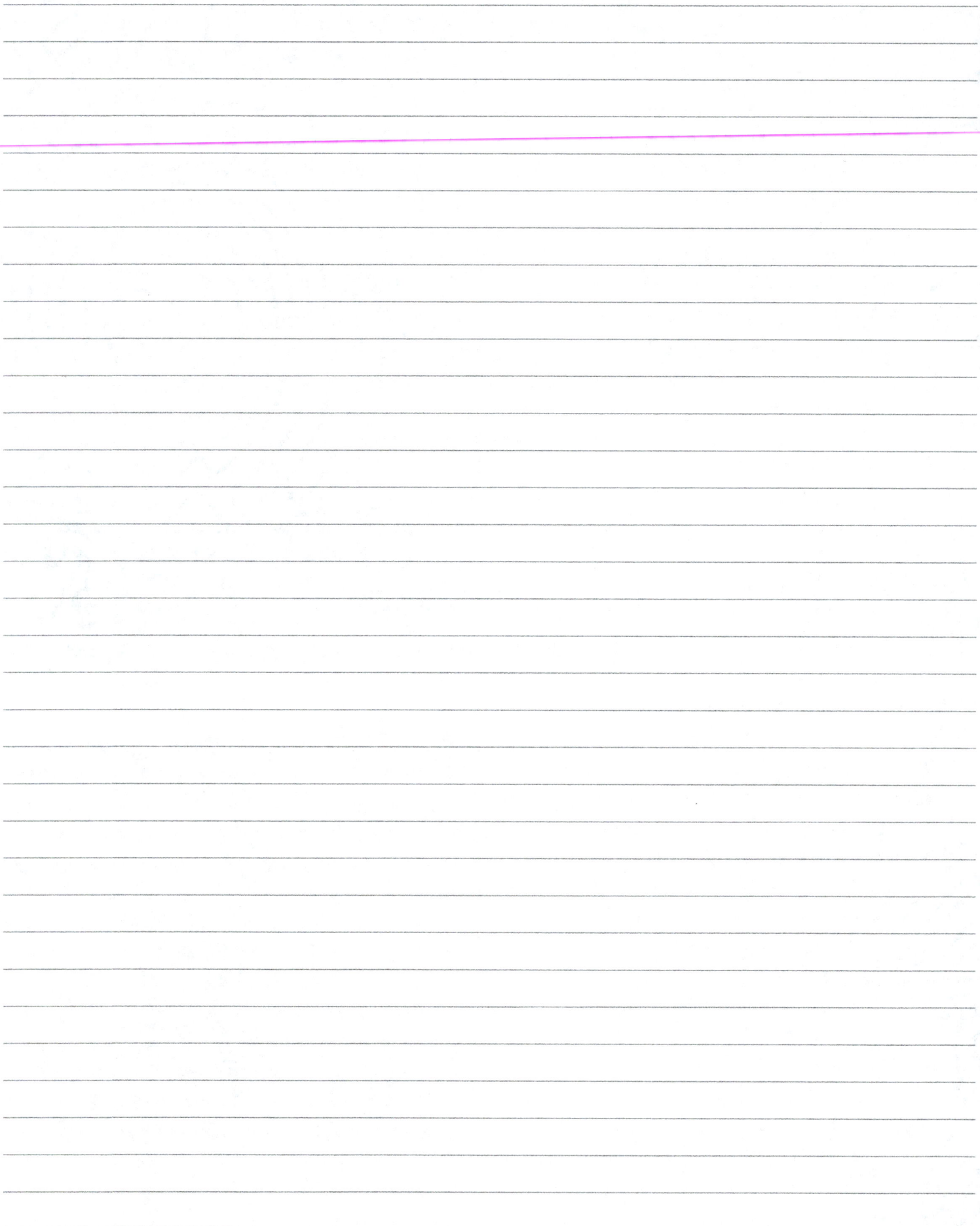

Never give up on anyone... Miracles happen every day

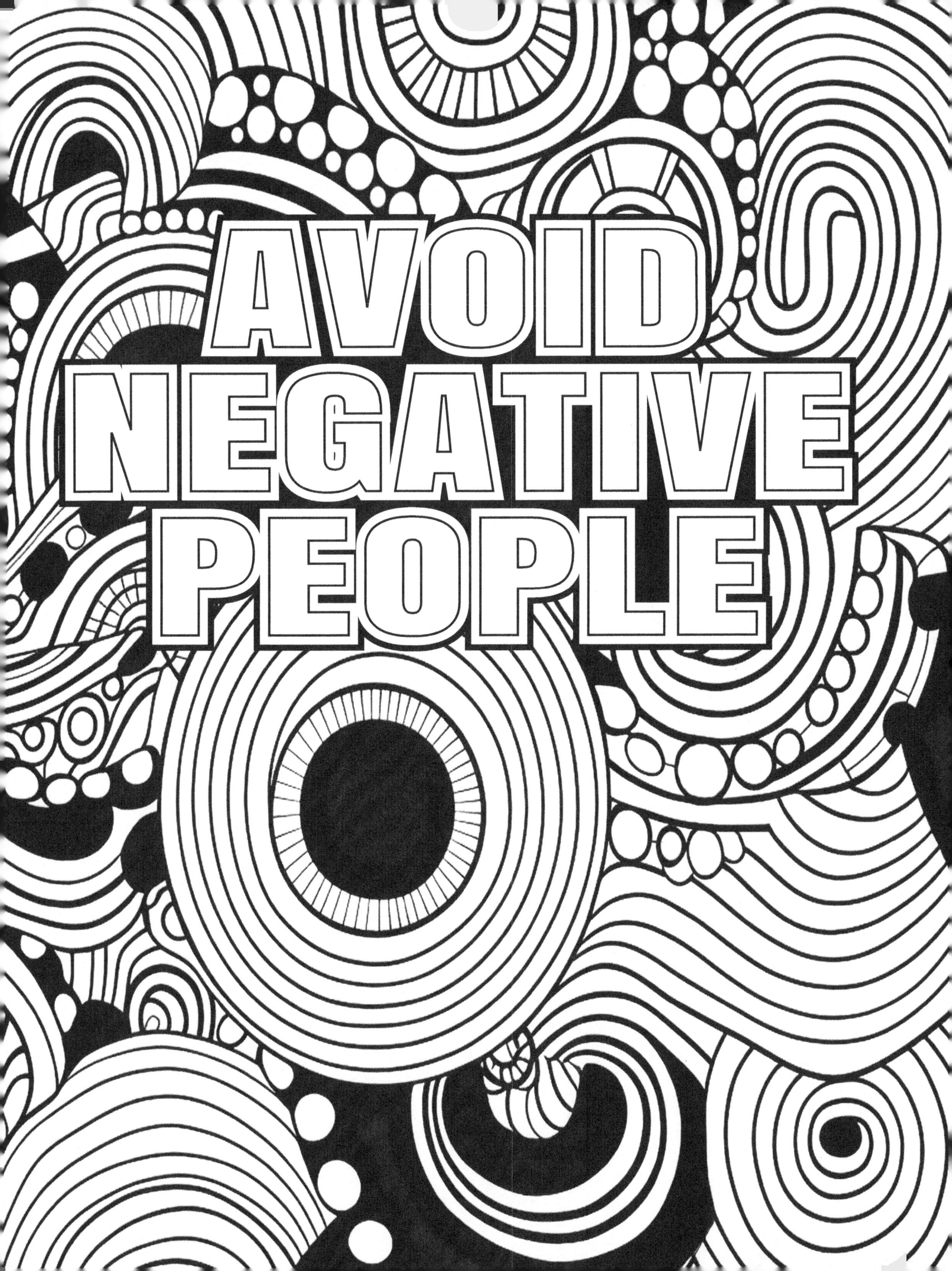
AVOID
NEGATIVE
PEOPLE

BE KINDER THAN NECESSARY

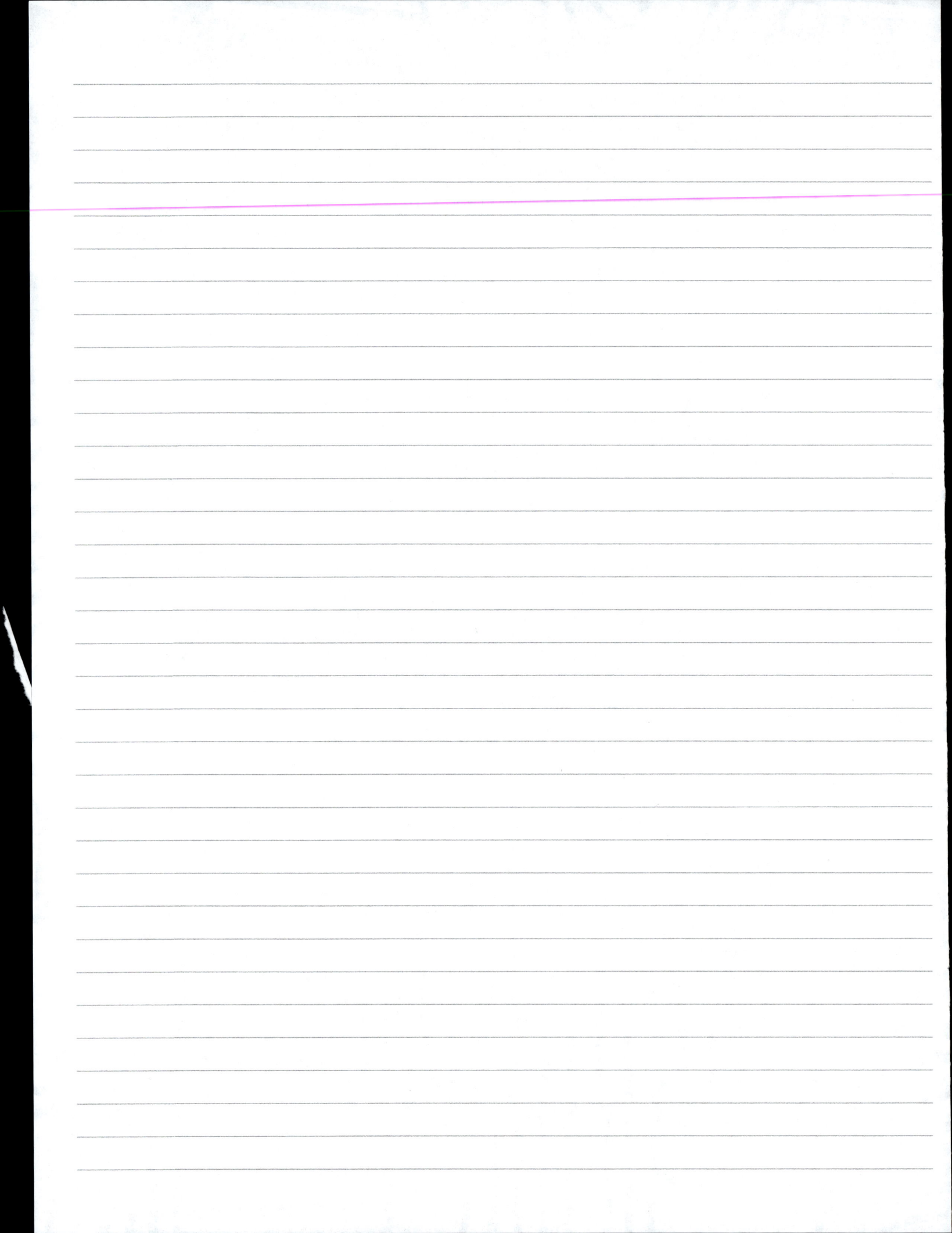

LEARN TO LISTEN
opportunity sometimes knocks softly

inner Peace

begins the moment you choose not to allow another person or event to control your emotions

start
each day
with a
grateful
heart

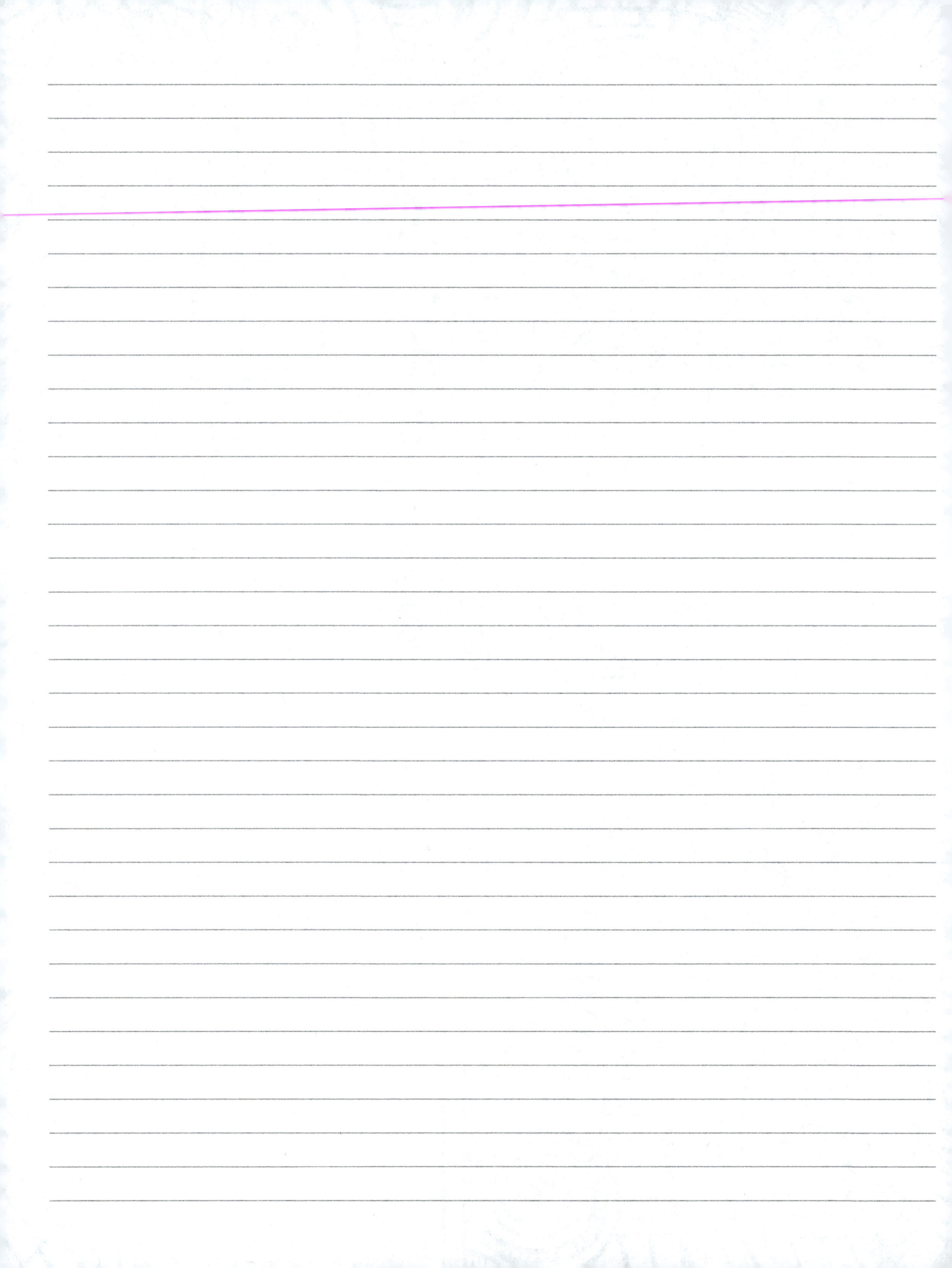

COMPARISON IS THE THIEF OF JOY

Theodore Roosevelt

it works if you work it
SO WORK IT
cause you're worth it!

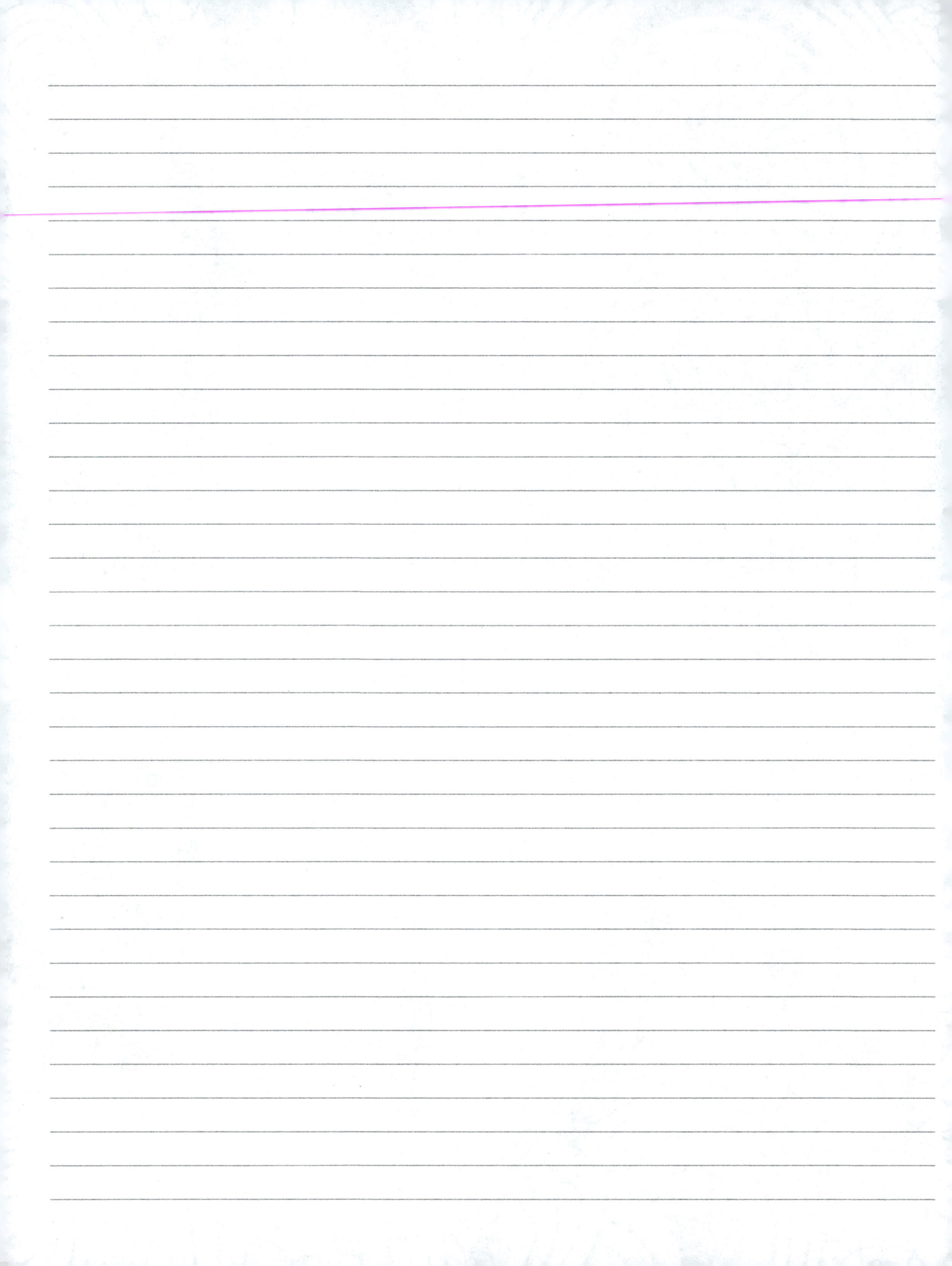

Religion
is for those who don't
want to go to hell;

Spirituality
is for those who have
already been there and
don't wish to return.

A.A. PHRASE

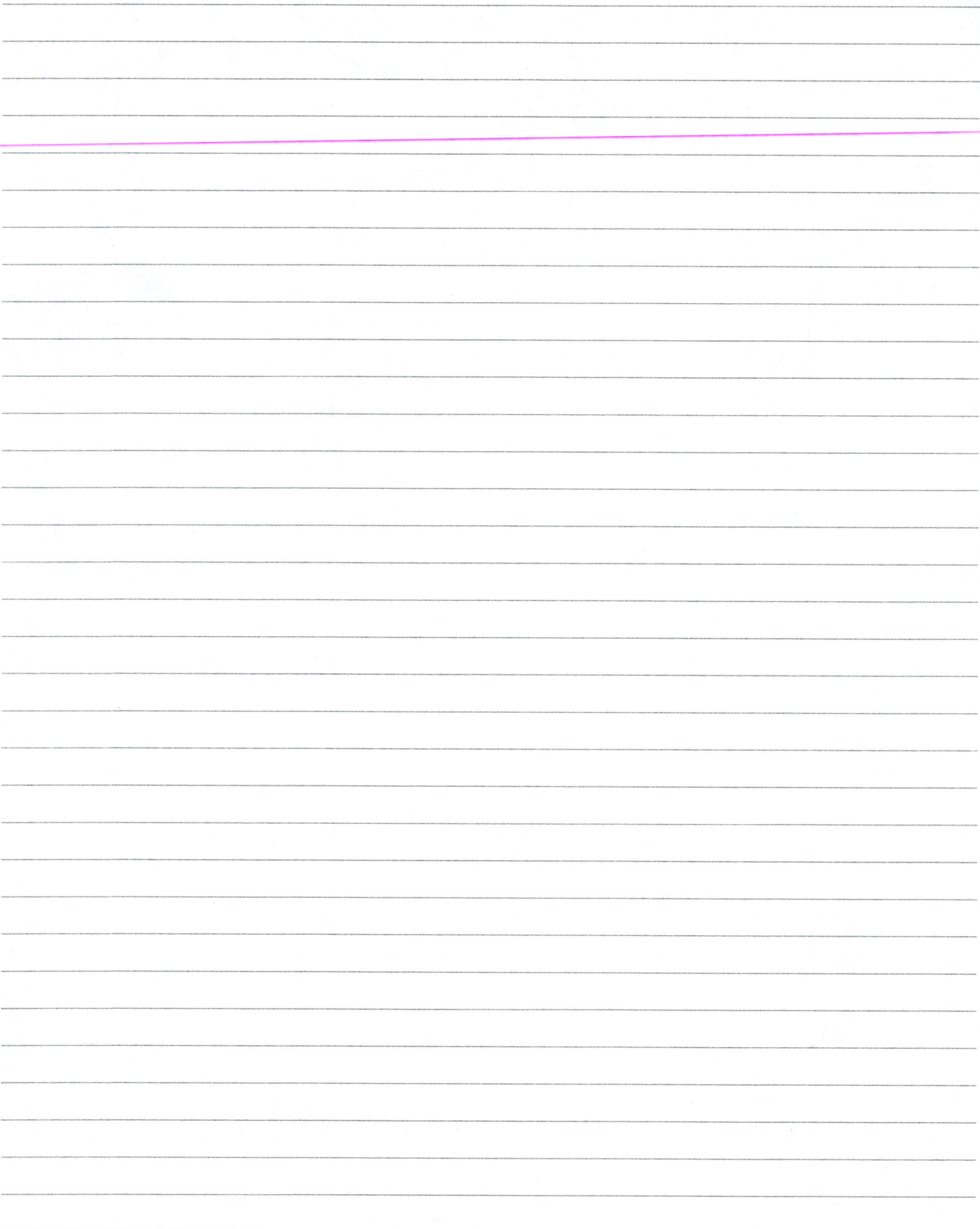

You have power over your mind – not outside events. Realize this, and you will find strength.

MARCUS AURELIUS

TRUST
GOD

CLEAN HOUSE

HELP
OTHERS

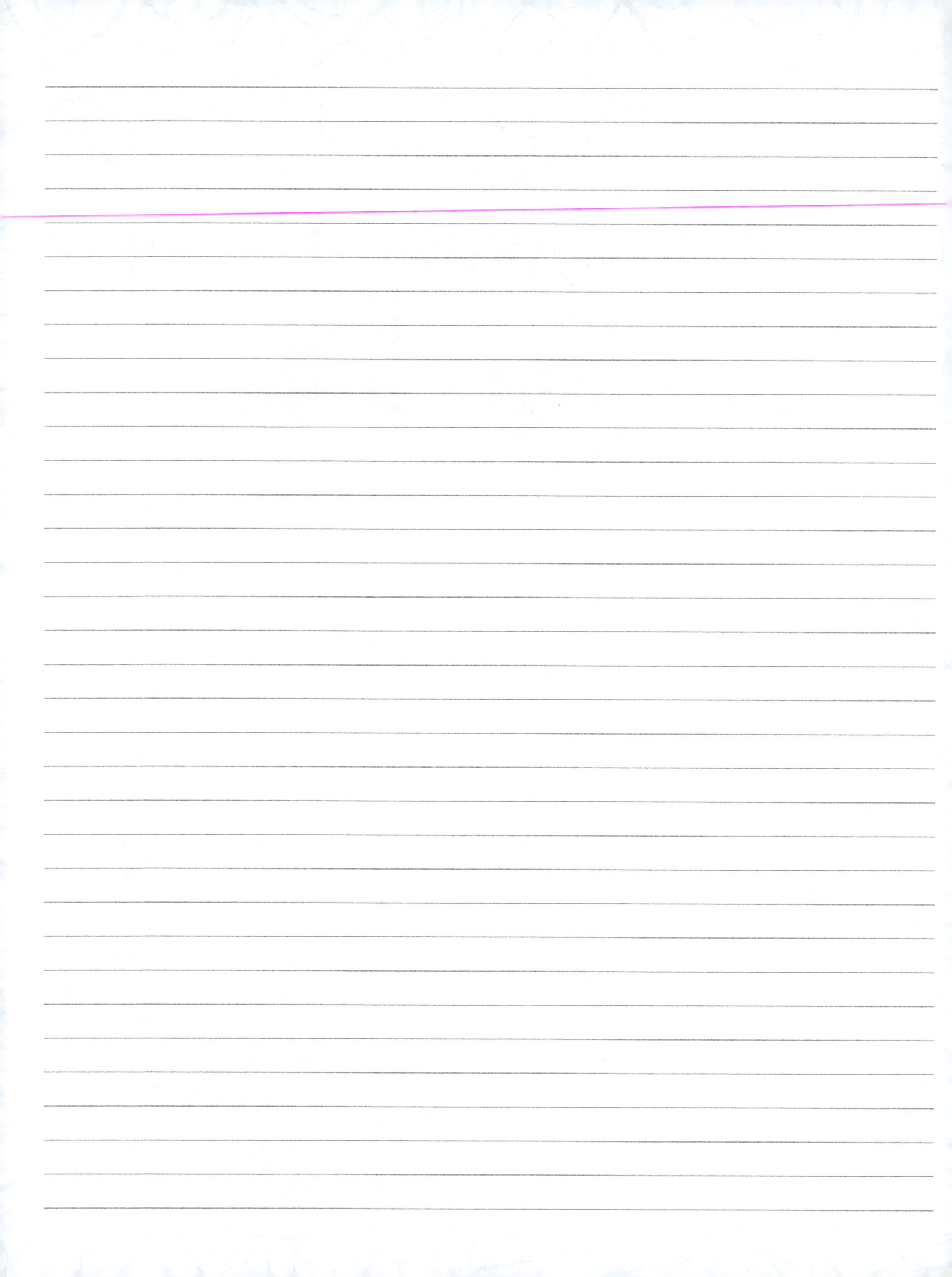

THE TWO MOST
IMPORTANT DAYS
IN YOUR LIFE
ARE THE DAY
YOU ARE BORN
AND THE DAY
YOU FIND OUT WHY.

MARK TWAIN

stay gold

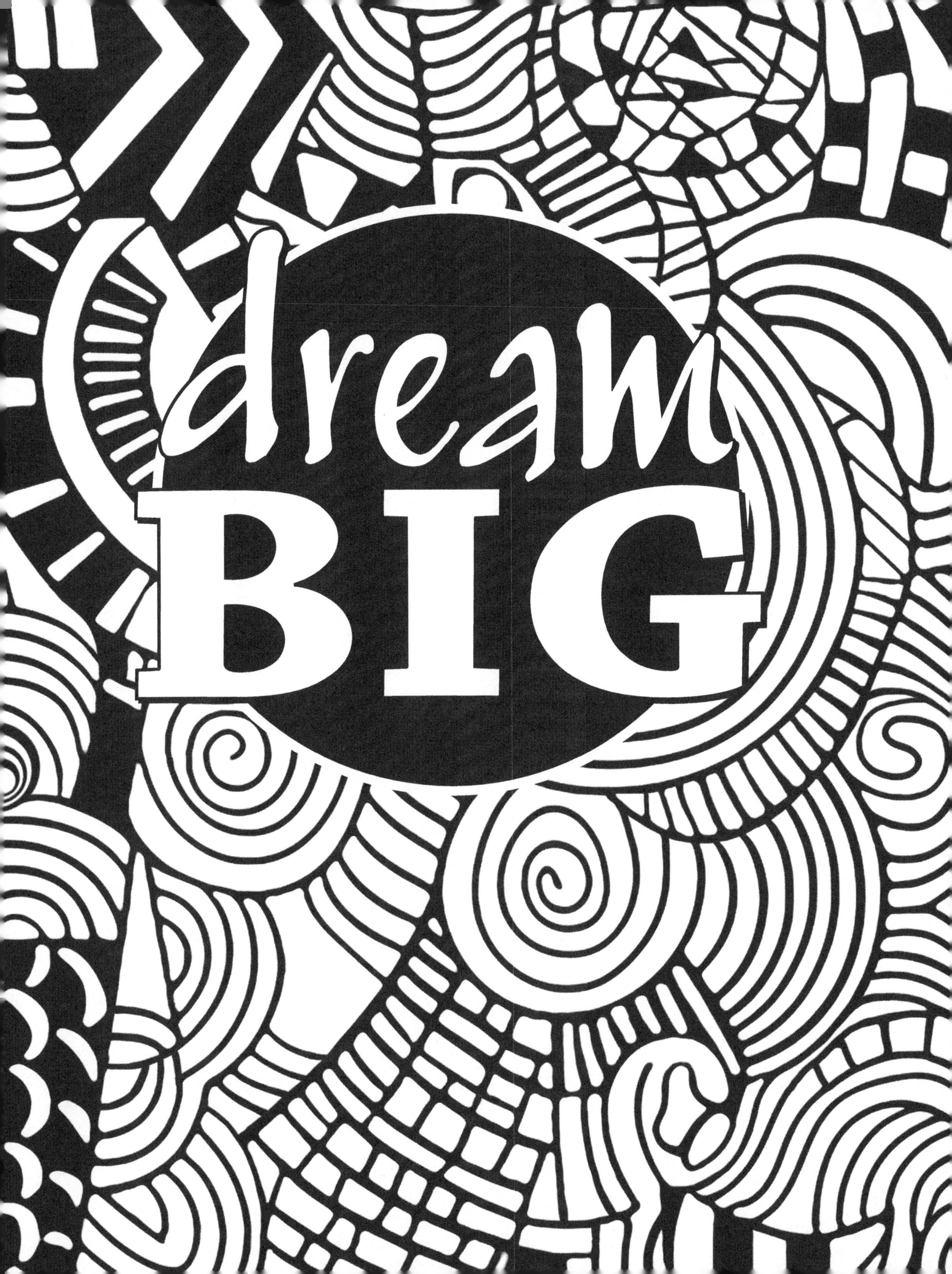
dream
BIG

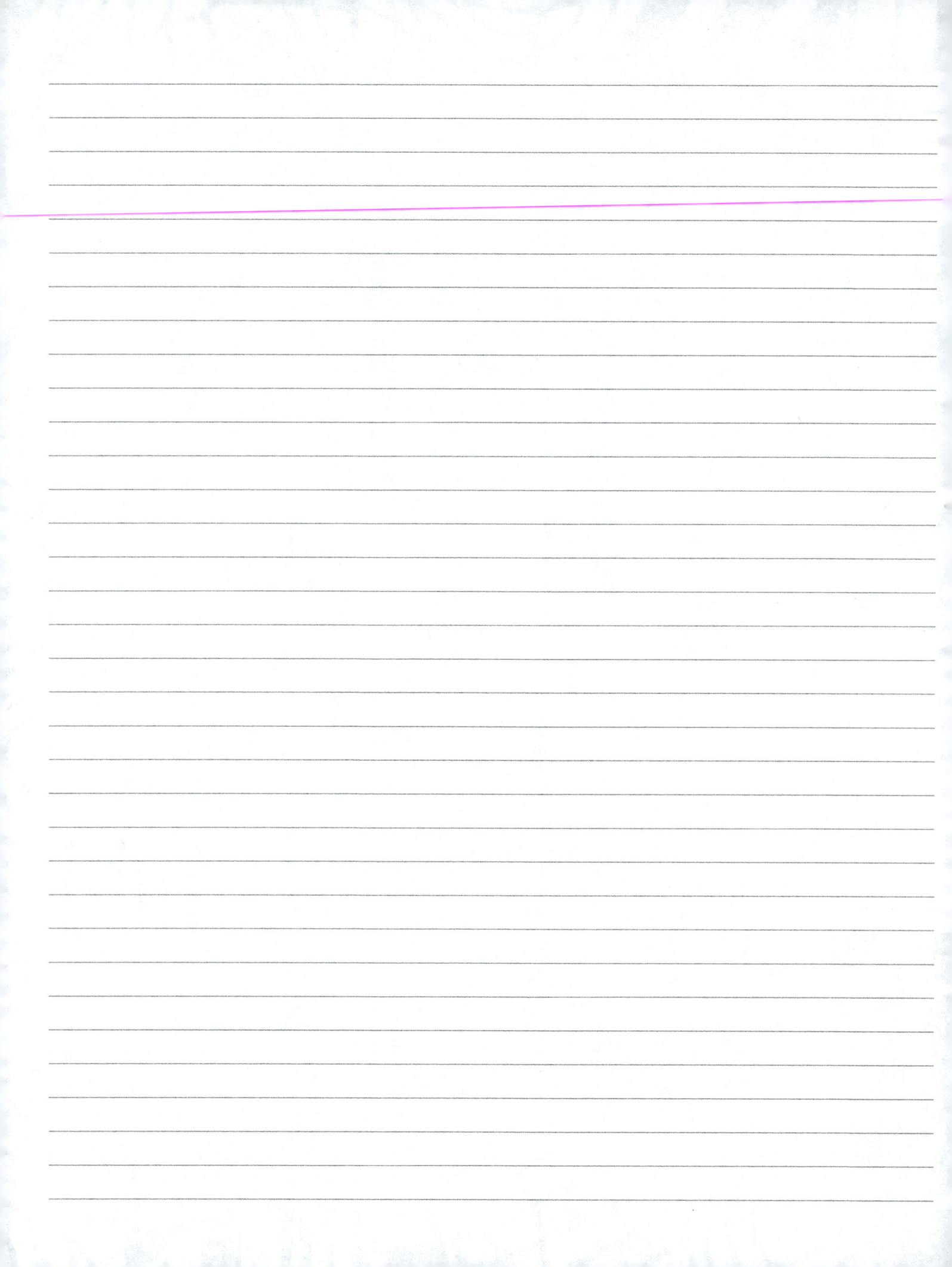

It's not
happiness that
brings you gratitude
———
It's gratitude that
brings you
happiness

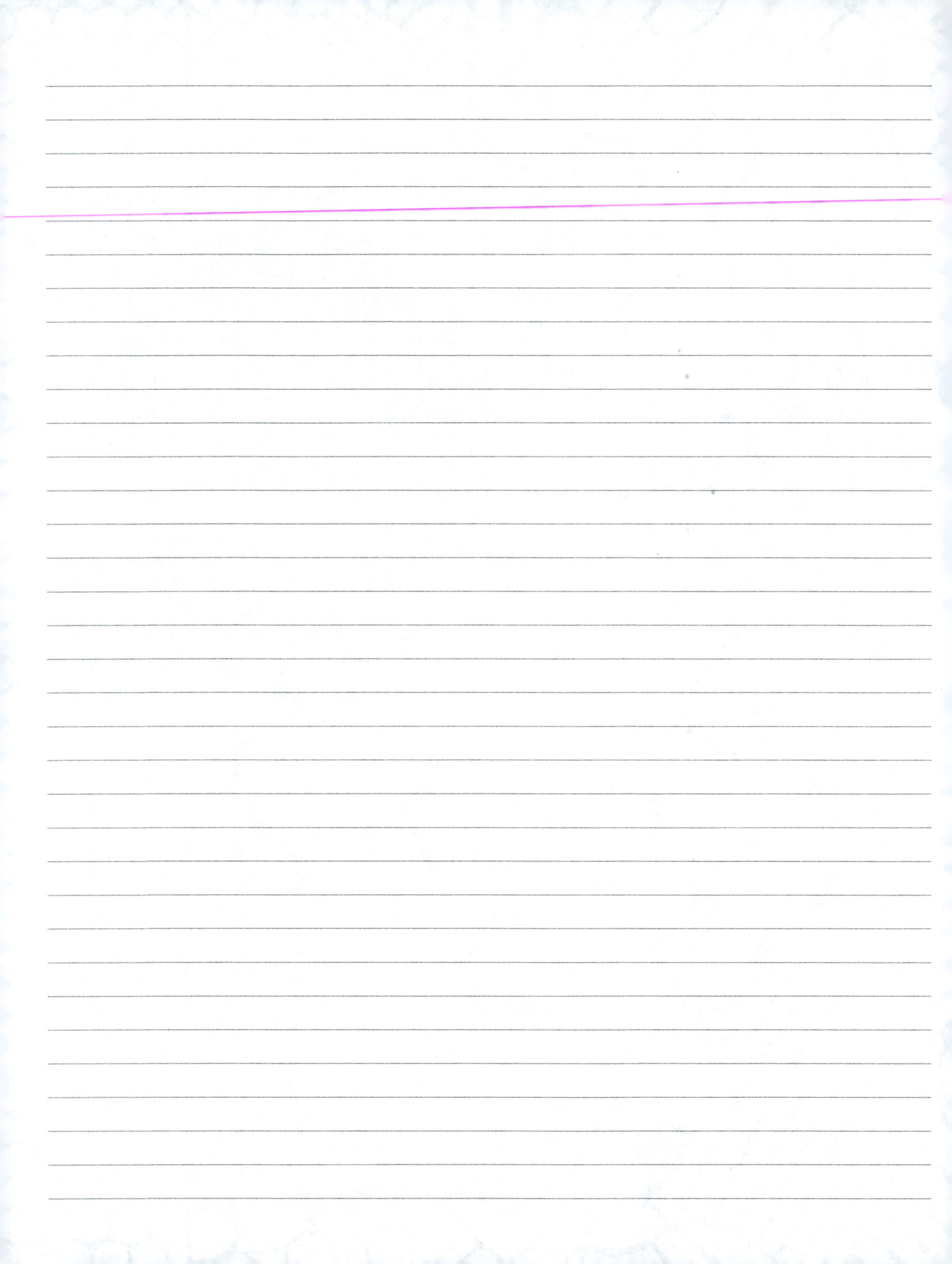

Discipline is choosing between what you want now and what you want most.

ABRAHAM LINCOLN

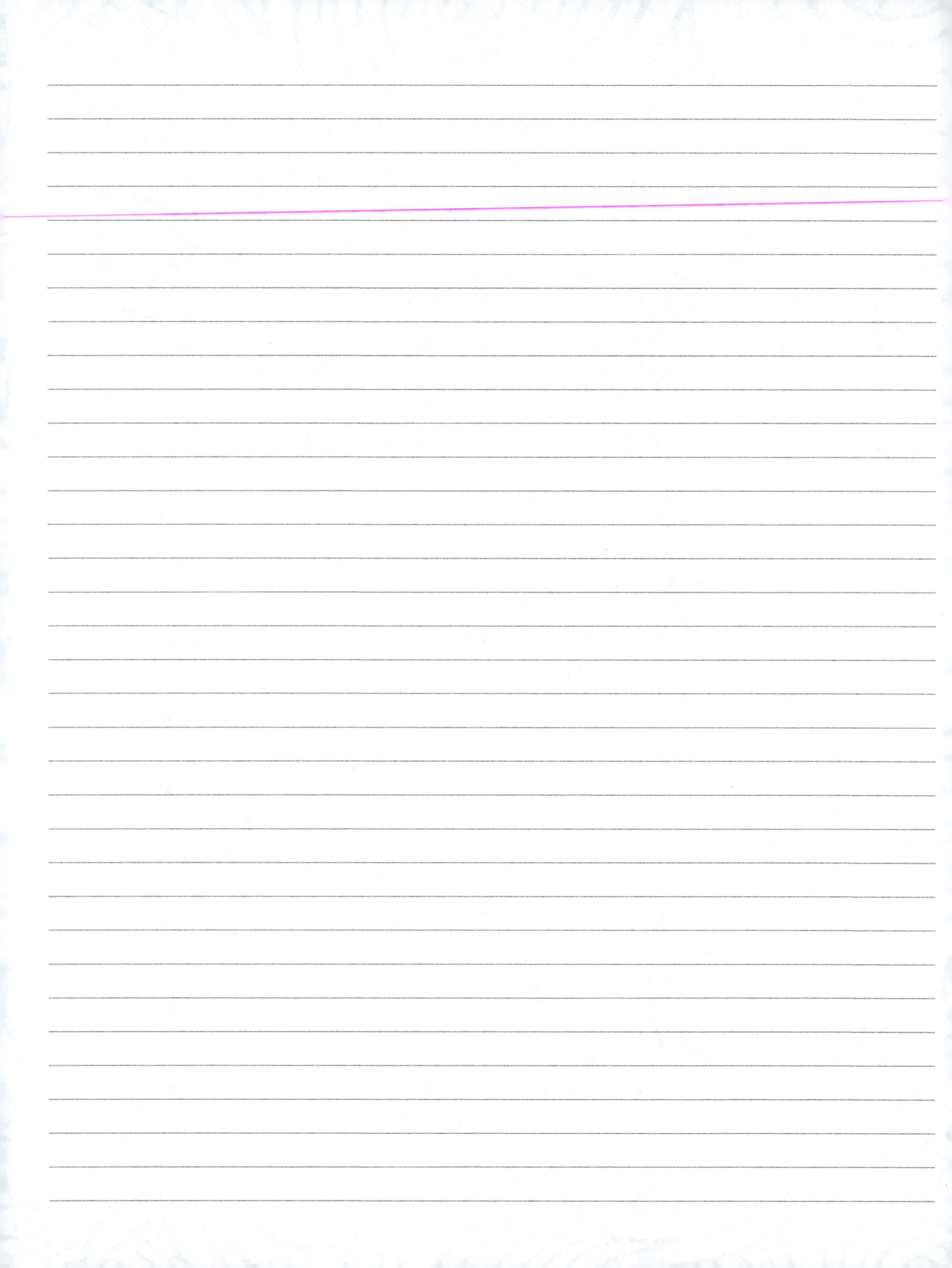

Don't waste time grieving over past mistakes.

Learn from them and move on.

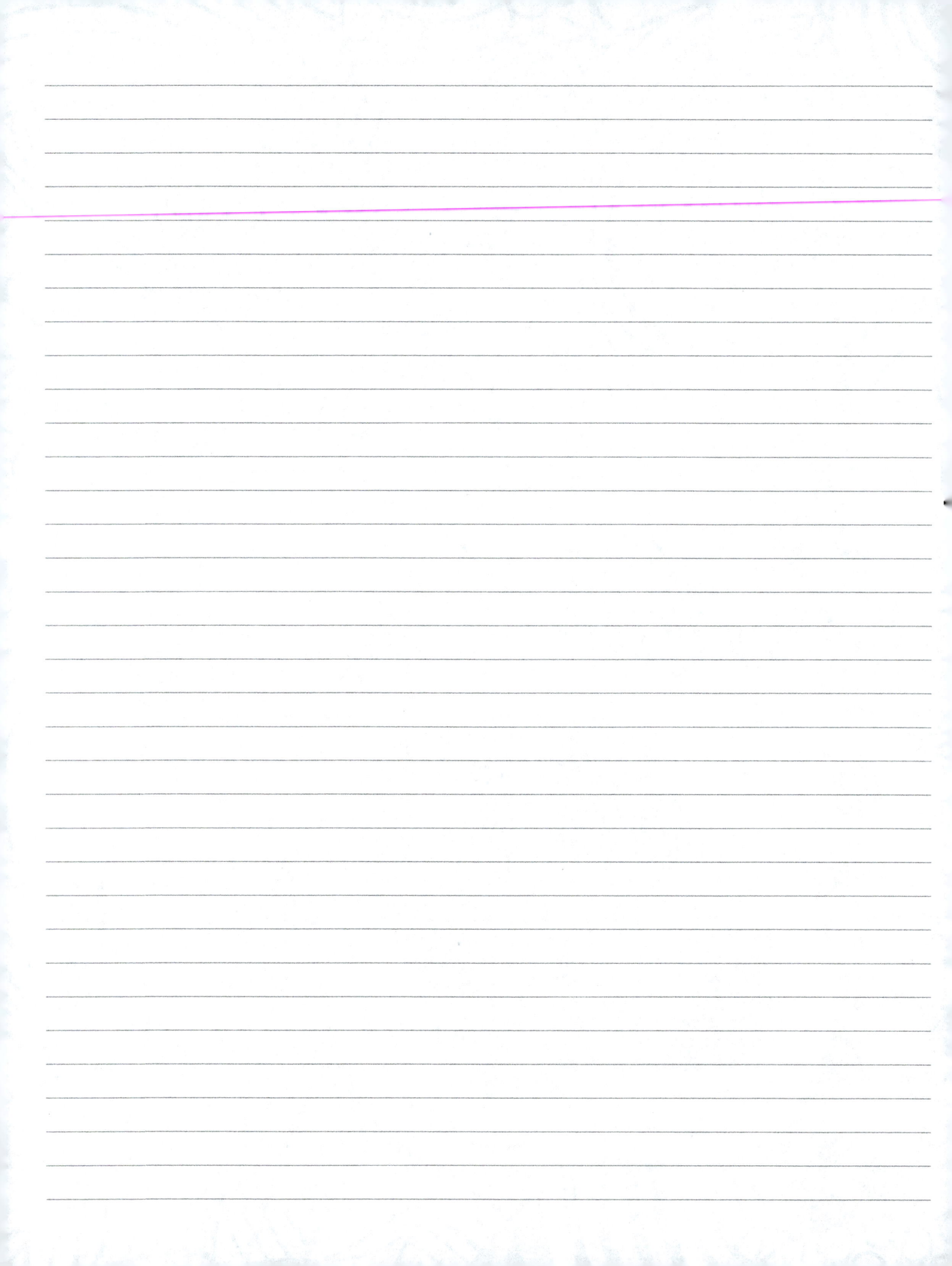

Perhaps this is the moment for which you have been created.

Esther 4:14

Made in United States
Orlando, FL
30 June 2025